PRAISE FOR MAKE YOUR AUTHOR EMPACT

"Stephanie Feger has leveraged her decade-long experience as a marketing and public relations expert to write a book aimed at helping authors make their voice heard above the noise. This powerful and dynamic book provides insight and inspiration to increase reach and impact with your valuable message. A 'must-read' for every author who wants to do more than just sell books."

Susan Friedmann, CSP
International Bestselling Author of *Riches in Niches: How to Make it BIG in a Small Market*

"This book is the complete guide to becoming an author. Stephanie helps you stand back and take the larger view. She gives you guideposts and unending encouragement to stay the course, and stay honest with yourself and the process. Each chapter is like tapping into a world-class coach."

Elisabeth Swan
Co-author of *The Problem-Solver's Toolkit*

"As a book coach and editor, one question I get over and over from authors is 'Now that I've written my book, how do I market it?' It's such a broad topic with so many potential paths depending on your book, your market, your goals. But now, with Stephanie's book, *Make Your Author emPact*, I have a resource to point them to that will walk authors through the steps needed to create their own author emPact. It's been a much longed for resource that I know I will turn to again and again."

Jennifer Crosswhite
Book Coach and Editor, Tandem Services

"An inspiring, insightful guide that connects the whole of what's inside each of us as authors (fear, insecurity, doubts, passion, perseverance, and joy) to bring a new perspective to the often daunting process of marketing a book. Powerful and empowering!"

Boni Wagner-Stafford
Author and Publisher at Ingenium Books

"If you're writing a book to grow your business, you need *Make Your Author emPact* in your life. Stephanie provides a practical toolkit of actionable steps to help authors build their brand and achieve their book marketing goals, no matter what stage of the publishing journey they're at. It provides everything an authorpreneur needs to create an effective marketing strategy to help them share their message, sell more books and achieve greater business success. I will be recommending it to all my author clients."

Jessica Brown
Nonfiction Book Editor

"At the time, my book launch was the most successful launch experienced by my publisher! I wrote the book; however, Stephanie built and maintained the momentum of its success! Her methodical approach to marketing directed (and encouraged) me to take steps designed to get the word out to the right people. With her guidance, she gifted me the tools to build visibility and spread the word. She understands the needs of authors and those of us who use a book as the foundation of a business. Thanks to her insights, my book accomplished the results I was seeking and I've continued sharing my message through speaking to college business classes and leadership teams and providing executive coaching with leaders of businesses. I encourage anyone who has interest in spreading the word about their book to read *Make Your Author emPact*. Why? Because I know the principles within work!"

Carson Sublett
Executive Coach and Author of *Bosses Are Hired ... Leadership is Earned*

"Many authors write their books without understanding that the most challenging part of the author journey is now in selling their books and creating impact. Stephanie Feger understands this and addresses this issue in her excellent new book, *Make Your Author emPact*.

As a marketing and PR expert, Stephanie shares her insights on authorpreneurship and provides practical advice for those who are in the throes of writing, as well as for those who have already published (and everyone in-between). She offers strategies and processes with energy and enthusiasm. Highly recommend."

Cathy Fyock
Author of *The Speaker Author*

"'I wrote a book—now what do I need to do?' Yep, that's a question I actually asked myself. And the answer was if I wanted to sell more books, if I wanted to share my message further, if I wanted to help more people, I'll need to market it. And luckily, I had Stephanie Feger to help me!

Stephanie helped provide me with everything I needed from whom I should market my book to, to what I need to make successful presentations, to building and maintaining a brand centered website to support it. And that's exactly what her book, *Make Your Author emPact: Sell More Books, Increase Your Reach & Achieve Your Why*, does for you—and more!

Stephanie's book gives you a comprehensive look at marketing to help you define and reach your goals. More importantly it gives you a map to follow on your own schedule. Her *emPact* on me helped me make greater *emPact* with my book—and this book will do the same for you!"

Wes Rutledge
Author of *So Dad, How Can I Make Dollars & Sense: Wealth-building Insights for When Adulting Begins in EARNest*

"Sitting down with Stephanie Feger's book, *Make Your Author emPact*, is like getting treated out to coffee by one of your best friends, clutching your warm mug between your hands as your best friend tells you that they one hundred percent know that you can accomplish all you have set out to conquer.

Her book asks the reader to look deep into themselves, diving head-first into self-discovery that will strengthen their writing and sharpen the will to persevere (because, as we know all too well, writing is hard).

While sharing anecdotes and learned experiences from her own writing and publishing journey, as well as providing keen insight into the vital (and often dreaded) realm of developing a marketing strategy for your book, this book shines a light into the murky waters of how to make sure your book is marketable, how to position yourself as a thought leader in your industry, all while proving that marketing is not a one-size-fits-all.

The wisdom learned from *Make Your Author emPact* will ensure that you never have to stumble along in the dark by providing manageable steps to determine what success means to you as well as opportunities for reflection; Stephanie's guidance provides guardrails to help keep the author on the right path for each individual book without over complicating the process.

Like your own personal cheerleader, *Make Your Author emPact* and Stephanie Feger believe in you, and are here to not just provide you with measured steps and actions to help get you from concept, to written book, to emPactful, published author, but to assure you that she believes in your success the whole way through."

Audrey Hoisington
Managing Editor, 2Nimble

"*Make Your Author emPact* is a must read for both seasoned authors as well as those putting pen to page for the first time. As an author of several books, I was surprised how much I didn't know about the actual book writing process let alone the book marketing and promotion process. The author quickly walks the reader through the process of writing her first book(s), gives readers good framework for defining *why* they might like to write a book and making sure they've unpacked what success of the book looks like before getting started. Then the author has a practical approach for planning, writing, publishing, launching and marketing of the book. Very well written and easy to read. I highly recommend it."

Dr. Joe DeSensi
President, Educational Directions

"You've always wanted to write a book, or you've written a book but don't know what to do with it now! If so, you need Stephanie Feger! Her new book, *Make Your Author emPact*, will guide you through the entire marketing process to success. Stephanie is authentic, inspiring, and truthful. She's been there and you'll know it. Her writing is conversational, her expertise in marketing is notable, and her practical advice is doable. You'll feel like you have your personal coach showing you the roadmap and walking along side you.

Whether you want to leave a legacy, make money, position yourself as a thought leader or grow your business… or all four reasons, through Stephanie's clear process you will create a powerful emPact on your own audience. You'll return to this book again and again!"

Elizabeth Jeffries, CSP, CPAE, MM
Executive Leadership Coach and Author of *What Exceptional Executives Need to Know: Your Step-by-Step Coaching Guide to Busting Communication Barriers, Keeping Top Talent & Growing Your Emerging Leaders!*

"I'm often asked what my secrets to a successful book launch and marketing efforts my bestselling book's first year and beyond are. The answer: Stephanie Feger. She was by my side from the months preceding my book's launch through to sustained impact over several years. Stephanie not only guided me in how to think and execute an 'emPactful' book marketing campaign, she also has been invaluable in supporting the 'emPact' of my professional brand as an author, speaker, and consultant. In the page of *Make Your Author emPact*, you'll learn the secrets behind Stephanie's approach and how you can make the emPact you want with your nonfiction book."

Katie Anderson
Leadership & Learning Coach and Author of *Learning to Lead, Leading to Learn: Lessons from Toyota Leader Isao Yoshino on a Lifetime of Continuous Learning*

MAKE YOUR AUTHOR EMPACT
SELL MORE BOOKS, INCREASE YOUR REACH & ACHIEVE YOUR WHY

STEPHANIE FEGER

STARGAZER
PUBLICATIONS

Make Your Author emPact: Sell More Books, Increase Your Reach & Achieve Your Why

Copyright © 2022 by Stephanie Feger
Published by Stargazer Publications (Kentucky)

All rights reserved. No portion of this book may be reproduced in any form or by electronic or mechanical means, including information storage and retrieval systems, without written permission of the author, except for the use of brief quotations in a book review.

Cover by Madelyn Copperwaite of MC Creative LLC
Editing by Jennifer Crosswhite of Tandem Services

First edition, September 2022
ISBN: 978-1-7363872-1-4
Library of Congress Control Number: 2022916654
Created in the United States of America

Learn more about Stephanie Feger and how the emPower PR Group can support you in your book marketing journey by visiting www.emPowerPRGroup.com. Special discounts are available on quantity book purchases. Contact info@empowerprgroup.com for information.

TABLE OF CONTENTS

Dedication	11
Your "One Day" is Today	13
Been There, Done That, and It's Time I Wrote a Book About It	17

PART ONE
YOUR AUTHOR EMPACT

1. Your Why Shapes Your How	25
2. You Determine Your Definition of Success	31
3. Guardrails and Road Marks	39
4. Create a Ripple	51
5. Don't Look Up, Look Down	57

PART TWO
WRITE A MARKETABLE BOOK

6. Do You *Need* The Brownies?	65
7. It's Not For You; It's For Them	75
8. You Are Bigger Than Your Book	83
9. The Difference Between a Writer and an Author	91
10. Don't Just Write It, Publish It	101

PART THREE
SELL MORE BOOKS

11. Building and Leveraging Your Author Platform	117
12. The Author's Social Dilemma	131
13. Ready. Set. Launch! (or Relaunch!)	139
14. emPowering Those Who Want You to Succeed	147
15. Get Seen. Be Heard. Sell Books.	157

PART FOUR
BUILD OR GROW A BUSINESS

16. A Book Can be the Beginning of a Business	167
17. The Authorpreneur Equation	175
18. Time Over Money or Money Over Time	183
19. The Bare Roots of Your Business	189
20. A Brisk Walk in the Park	197

PART FIVE
EMPOWERED AUTHORS LEAVE AN EMPACT

21. emPower with a Capital P	209
22. Don't Think Differently, Think Different	215
23. Be the Tortoise Not the Hare	219
24. When You Know, You Can't Unknow	225
25. Your Book is Not a Banana	231
Books Build Bridges and Break Down Walls	235
A Special Gift from Me to You	239
Now That You're emPowered…	241
Acknowledgments	245
About The Author	249
About the emPower PR Group	251
Also by Stephanie Feger	253

DEDICATION

We all deserve to have someone believe in us—in our dreams, in our passions, in our possibilities and in our stories. This book is dedicated to those who have a story the world needs and a dream within them that has been stirred up by their passions. I believe when you follow your dream, your life is full of possibilities. Whether those around you believe your story is worthy of being shared or that you have an idea with the potential to change lives, communities or even the world—whether *you* believe it is possible or not—know I believe in you.

Every story matters, including yours.

To those who have tried to shake a dream that feels unattainable but just can't…

To those who feel called to share their story with others but haven't uncovered how to make it happen…

To those who have a dream to accomplish something big but are afraid to take the next step…

To those who feel immobilized by what that next step should be and don't know who to trust to help guide them…

To those who are ready to share their message but haven't a clue how to…

To those who are ready to take a big leap of faith but are a bit nervous where they might land…

It's okay. My hand is stretched out. I'm ready to guide and support you as you make your author emPact.

This book is dedicated to you. Your story and your message is needed in this world. Don't ever question it. Take that leap. It is worth it.

YOUR "ONE DAY" IS TODAY

I had a goal and starting a business wasn't it.

In fact, my husband was the one with the entrepreneurial spirit. I envisioned him launching his own physical therapy practice where I would be *his* cheerleader. I never considered the reverse scenario. I had a solid career… one that was about making a difference instead of just making money. I felt fulfilled. What more could I want?

I never *wanted* more, not until *it* happened.

A dream. Literally. An occurrence many brush off with the dawn of a new day set my life down a path of unexpected detours. A simple message delivered as a gift in a nighttime escape. I awoke with the charge to write a book.[1]

Much like how I felt about starting a business, I felt the same about becoming an author. Didn't most authors grow up with the dream of becoming one? That wasn't me. I *had* enjoyed writing my whole life. Writing monologues for theater auditions were my childhood specialty, and I had built a career on using my writing skills to help businesses and organizations promote their messages through public relations, marketing and communications strategies. Writing I enjoyed… but writing a book I wasn't so sure of.

The day following my dream was the day I started jotting down thoughts for a book I was destined to write... some day. I just didn't know it yet. A bucket-list item Life had decided for me without my permission. One day, in the unforeseen future, it would come to fruition when Life knew the time was right.

But I had other priorities.

I was working more hours than I'd care to admit and, at the same time, my husband and I were focused on growing our family. We schlepped through life with diaper bags, runny noses, bags under our eyes and three little kiddos to attribute to them. There are only so many hours in the day, and my hours were taken up by a job and a family. There was little room for anything else.

But, behind closed doors, Life giggled. Life had a plan and without my knowing or approval was drafting a new page each day in a book I *would* write. And, as with most things, when Life is ready for you to take action, you may not be. I know I wasn't.

For years, I looked at writing as an escape. It brought me solace. During the depths of pregnancy insomnia and early morning reprieves, I would write when I was inspired and couldn't sleep. But after an unexpected sequence of events, my charge to write and publish a book could no longer be ignored. My story needed to be shared. I decided to go all in.

Life had won.
It was time.

IT HAD BEEN "ONE OF THOSE" WEEKS.

You may commiserate. You have all of your ducks in a row, and yet you never get the opportunity to tackle your ducks. Each day I hoped for a better outcome, but Life scoffed at my goals. By Friday, all of my kids had snotty noses and concerning coughs, and this momma was holding it together by merely a thread. A thread that frayed the moment I walked into the pediatrician's office.

The doctor stayed late that day to evaluate my youngest, but when she walked into the exam room, she focused on me instead. She saw something I had hoped I could hide, but I have a terrible poker face and my façade shattered. I was struggling to be good at everything, only to feel like I was good at nothing. So when she opened her mouth to ask about me, I couldn't stop waterworks from taking over. Within minutes, she put down her stethoscope and did something many in her field wouldn't have… she invited me to a Bible study.

I went, unsure what to expect as I had never been to one before, but by the fourth week I knew I needed to share something I hadn't with anyone else. That evening, I nervously held a few pieces of paper and glided into the room trying to exude the confidence I wished I had. I tiptoed to the podium and, for the first time, I read aloud a chapter of a book I had been writing in secret. A book I had been charged to write from a dream.

Unexpectedly, this leap of faith was the first step in writing and publishing my first book, launching two businesses and a journey to supporting others who would one day have the courage to also take that leap, but this time with my hand to guide them.

Vulnerability took the lead that night as I cautiously shared a piece of me no one else knew about, and when I made my way back to my chair, I found a note for my eyes only awaiting. A woman in the group had jotted down the name of the person who would guide me to fulfill my life's new mission. The contact information for a book coach was on the ripped piece of lined notebook paper, but it took me months to muster up the courage to meet her.

My husband could hear it in my voice the moment I called him on my way home from my initial consultation. I had found new energy and a passion had been sparked. He could tell a shift was happening. Long before I accepted it, he knew becoming an author (and later, an authorpreneur) was in my future, and it would all start with me believing my story was worthy of being shared.

THAT DAY WAS MY "ONE DAY."

It's ingrained in my memories—alongside marrying my best friend and the birth of our three kids—as a cornerstone moment that shifted my life's trajectory. It set off a domino effect, leading me through experiences that shaped me, refined me and later became the defining elements of a business I would build called the emPower PR Group. One action has power, and the beginning of my book journey was *that* action for me. It may be for you too.

Today may be your "one day." It may be what spawns your defining moments.

Maybe today you make the conscious decision to write the book you've always wanted to (or the one you can't seem to run away from, the one begging to be shared).

Maybe today you decide it's time to launch or relaunch your book and ensure those who desperately need your message (and will pay for it) know it exists.

Maybe today you realize your book was destined to be lifted off the pages and invited into the lives of others.

Maybe today is the day you decide to create a meaningful business from your book's emPowering messages.

One day is all you need to get started. And that one day can start now.

---

1. And writing a book, I did. My first book, *Color Today Pretty: An Inspirational Guide to Living a Life in Perspective*, outlines this pivotal moment in my life and the shift in how I saw myself in the process.

BEEN THERE, DONE THAT, AND IT'S TIME I WROTE A BOOK ABOUT IT

When asked what I wanted to be when I grew up, I would always land on one of three career paths: veterinarian, teacher or actress. While I didn't formally choose any of these careers, the core elements of each found their way into my life:

- I may not be a formal teacher (although the pandemic pushed me into homeschooling), but I do get to teach authors, speakers, authority brands and thought leaders marketing insights.
- I traveled to Los Angeles, California, with the hopes of getting "discovered" but instead discovered that the confidence found on an acting stage doesn't have to stay there. It can be transferred onto other stages, like a speaking stage or a podcast platform.
- While I sure do love animals, I decided to stick to fostering them (and having a mini zoo of our own).

Writing a book and becoming an author wasn't something I planned to tackle, so when I felt the calling to do so, I wasn't sure where to start. My first step was saying "yes" to attending a Bible study. From there, the path unfolded—step-by-step—as I navigated unexplored terrain.

At least, it was unexplored for me, but many others had been there, done that and were ready to guide me.

There's this unspoken rule in the book industry. **When you need help, someone will be there to help you. And when someone else needs help, you should be there to help them too.** It's a pay-it-forward belief that is interwoven in its DNA. And it's my goal of writing this book.

Help was there when I needed it most. Sometimes it came in the form of a wrinkled piece of paper, the name of a book coach scrawled across it. Other times, it was in a coffee chat, a YouTube video or someone willing to take a chance on me. Today, I want to be your help, and if you want my help beyond this book, holler.[1]

I'VE BEEN THERE.

Before diving into all things book marketing, it's important to share some pivotal moments in my own book journey so when I tell you I've been there, you know it's true.

Once my goal became clear, it felt like nothing was going to stand in my way. But the day I met the woman who would soon become my book coach, I left with a mix of emotions. I was eager to write and publish a book, but I couldn't imagine how I would make it happen. Financially.

I was working full-time, as was my husband, but I decided my book would not be funded by the money meant to support our family of five. Not that I don't support funding a dream in this capacity, but I knew I had another route I needed to take—an additional journey that would end up being important to who I was becoming. (Remember how Life works? Yeah, Life was putting in overtime.)

I didn't plan on becoming an entrepreneur, but that Christmas was the kickstart to another "new" for me... running a business.

Twas the season, and a family member had just moved into a new home. I decided to gift them with what anyone would gift a new homeowner during the holidays... a wreath! Right?! Isn't that something you would think of too? For those who know me now, this would come as no surprise, but those who knew me then would question why I had chosen to not just purchase a wreath but *make* one. Good question. I had no real answer other than I wanted to.

The only problem was I had never made a wreath before. Well, the year prior I threw some floral picks into a pre-made Christmas pine wreath for our front door, but outside of that debacle, I had never ventured into wreath making. While the odds were against me, when I get an idea, I can't shake it until I try it. I ventured to the nearest craft store and collected what experts on the YouTube videos told me I would need. With spools of burlap, white hydrangea floral picks and endless floral wire in hand, nothing was going to stop me.

My first wreath was quite a beauty or at least I thought so. So much so that I opted to make two more as gifts for other family members. Upon completion of the third, I had started to get the hang of it, and I was quite proud of what I had accomplished. I sat there, admiring my creations, and decided to do what any excited person would upon conquering such a feat. I took a photo and posted it on social media. I couldn't celebrate independently! I had to share.

I expected to get a few likes and a couple of comments, nothing major. But one comment caught my attention.

"Beautiful! Do you sell these?"

It was a good question. I hadn't considered it since I had just learned how to make them. I was proud of my work and definitely thought they were eye-catching, but I knew nothing about the craft or how to run a business, so merging the two was a particularly daunting idea. I was wanting to write a book, not launch a business. Ugh!

I'm glad I didn't question myself for long and dove into a side hustle of wreath making. As it turned out, within six months I had not just raised enough money to self-fund the publishing of my first book, I had also created a business full of potential. A business that provided an opportunity for me to become an entrepreneur (and later help others—including authors—do the same).

Within the first year, I fine-tuned my skills and shaped my business. Within two years, and through a mixture of custom designs and workshops, over a thousand custom wreaths adorned doors across the nation. A moment of creativity, which had begun as a gift-making effort, provided my dream financial stability, gave my soul a creative outlet and was the beginning of my author platform.

Along my journey, I took notes of what worked well and what fell flat. I had days of success and days where I begged my husband to massage my cramping hands. Nothing about my journey was easy, but everything about it was fulfilling. Nestled within the pages of this book you will hear more of how a single wreath and a dream changed everything.

It pushed me to write a book.
It emPowered me to launch that book to success.
And it taught me what I needed to build a business from a passion
(and later, launch a second one to help others, just like you).

When I say I understand you, I do. I understand where you are because I've been there. And as an author myself, I've done firsthand what I'm going to teach you in the pages ahead.

THERE'S ONE MORE FACTOR I HAVEN'T QUITE TOUCHED ON, AND I THINK IT'S AN IMPORTANT ONE.

By trade, I'm not an author (or at least I wasn't until I published in 2018). My academic and professional background is in public relations, communications and marketing. I worked in the nonprofit and agency industries for over 15 years before publishing my first book. Launching the book was more exciting to me than writing it, if I'm being honest, because of my background and skillset. I knew how to market my book, but my publishing team didn't know the marketing side of me yet.

Before my book's launch, my book coach requested I present my launch plan to her coaching cohort. I pulled my thoughts together and in the middle of my favorite cafe, I put on my headset and did a virtual presentation on my plan. Immediately after my presentation, my phone rang. My book coach and my publisher were wanting to connect with me. And pronto.

I thought I was in trouble.
It turned out to be quite the opposite.

Both asked how I came up with my launch strategy, and I reminded them marketing was what I went to school for, not writing. Marketing was my jam. They informed me that, for most authors, it wasn't theirs.

That day I learned a group of amazing people with game-changing messages consistently found themselves lodged between writing a book and marketing it. Most would rather clean toilets than engage in marketing activities. (I'm serious. I've had an author literally express that sentiment to me!)

That itch I had to publish a book challenged me to merge my unique expertise with my life's passions. I've always wanted to help others share their skills with the world. I've always worked to emPower people who sought to emPower others. Now, as an author and authorpreneur, I decided to bring my marketing, communications and public relations skills to your unique needs and help you reach your goals!

The emPower PR Group was born.

Together with a team of highly skilled marketing experts, we blend personal experience with innovative marketing solutions to ensure those who need to hear of a message, a book, an author or a brand, do!

That book I wrote—the one that changed my career trajectory—just so happened to be about perspective, and perspective is my secret sauce. In fact, it's a perfect complement to emPowerment. And it's at the very heart of this book.

---

1. I offer complementary chats with authors, and I would love to, well, chat! Visit emPowerPRGroup.com to schedule one.

PART ONE
YOUR AUTHOR EMPACT

author emPact (n): the emPowering effect of an author's message that inspires action, ignites change and makes a difference in the lives of many

CHAPTER 1
YOUR WHY SHAPES YOUR HOW

As an author and a book marketing expert, I find this statistic to be accurate: over 80 percent of Americans feel they have a book in them that is calling to be written, published and shared![1]

That's exciting! Especially since I know, firsthand, how stories (and books) and writers (and authors) change lives in very meaningful, real and impactful ways. But what I find even more interesting are their reasons *why* they are writing a book in the first place.

Pause for a moment and consider *why* you want to write a book (or why you already have). In a world with a multitude of ways to communicate, have you considered *why* writing a book is your method of choice?

It's a **time commitment**. There's no running from that.

It's a **financial investment**. No matter your publishing approach, there will always be money involved, no matter your goals.

It requires **persistence, dedication and commitment**. Let's be real, writing a book is a massive undertaking. One that pairs well with exhaustion and overwhelm. It's a vulnerable experience, exposing your perspective, your stories and yourself in the process.

To others, the list of *why not*s may be enough to trade in their pen and quit before they've even begun. But there's a reason you haven't. There's a reason you have taken on a challenge so many have attempted and so few have accomplished. Understanding that reason can help you determine your marketing needs.

YOUR WHY TELLS A STORY.

I've had the pleasure of meeting and working with countless authors. It's become one of my favorite pastimes. Each author is as unique as their story. And each author's process of writing, publishing and marketing their book fascinates me. I'm on the verge of needing more bookshelves to house all the signed books that I've collected over the years. If I'm going to collect something, why not author-signed books?!

While each author's story is nuanced and laced with personal experiences, I've uncovered a commonality and it comes down to their *why*. I've found that most authors can be categorized into one of three *why* buckets.

The author wants to **share a message, make a difference and/or make money**.

Now, you may be thinking, "But Stephanie, I want to do all three. Why would I write a book if I didn't want to tell someone something, leave a lasting impact or get rich quick?!" Yes, I realize this is an *and/or* not an *either/or* situation, but hear me out. At the root of why you wrote your book (or are writing your book) there's a single most important reason. I know this because I had a *why* too.

I DON'T CARE IF I HAVE 500 COPIES IN MY BASEMENT.

That's what I told my husband after I realized why I was writing my first book, *Color Today Pretty*.

My *why* slipped out of me as if I'd felt the need to convince him what I was doing was worthwhile, but he needed no convincing. He was on board well before I accepted this challenge. When I confidently stated my why, I was really convincing *myself*.

I had an itch to write a book. It started like a small bug bite you don't know you have until you've scratched it so much your skin turns red and raw—yelling for help, moisturizer and anti-itch cream. It wasn't going to stop until I made my book a reality. But I couldn't figure out *why* I needed to write it until I spoke my *why* out loud.

I didn't write my book to become the next millionaire, which was good because most authors never come close to reaching that accolade. I didn't write my book to go on a speaking tour or form a business from it. I didn't write my book to reach the masses. I now know that if you try to reach everyone, you will reach no one.

I wrote my book for the *one*—for that one person who needed to hear what I needed to hear. And, if I'm being honest, I was that person. Initially, I wrote my book for *me*.

With each chapter I drafted, I was filled with a mix of vulnerability and peace. I knew the book was an act of catharsis. And I knew someone else needed it too. I just didn't know who quite yet.

So, I walked up to my husband and boldly told him, if no one buys my book, that's okay because *I* need the message in my book. In fact, if I have 500 copies of it in my basement, that's okay, too, because I have proven to my kids that you can do anything you set your mind to.

Of course, there is a lot of flawed thinking in my declaration to my husband; I just didn't know that yet. Lucky for me, I learned that thanks to print on demand publishing, I didn't have to have 500 copies in my basement.

KNOWING YOUR WHY HELPS DEVELOP YOUR MARKETING PLAN.

As excited as I was to write my book, I was even more excited to market it. Had I known the power of the Author emPact Framework[2] when my first book was published, I could have saved myself hours by focusing my marketing efforts to align with my *why*.

I realize now it's just that simple.

Through my work with authors, I've discovered understanding someone's *why* will also help identify the most effective and strategic marketing efforts. This is important because it **saves time**, it **saves resources** and it **saves energy**. In a world where new marketing opportunities seem as endless as the colors of M&M candies (go to the M&M store in Orlando, Florida, and you'll have a brain explosion moment), it's important to make movements with strategy. And that just happens to be one of my mottos.

Your *why* matters and so does your book.

Even though I know most people who dream of writing a book may never complete that bucket-list goal, I continue to be amazed hearing their whys:

"I have a message I think could make a difference."
"I *need* to share this story."
"I want to help people who are struggling."
"My experiences have purpose. Maybe I can help someone else."
"I'm ready to quit my nine-to-five. And a book will help me do that."
"I want to leave a legacy."
"I want to inspire others in ways I can't do otherwise."
"I want to prove to myself I can."
"I want to show the world I can do anything."
"I want to build a new income stream."
"I'm ready to be seen as *the* subject matter expert in my field!"
"It seems selfish not to share what I know."
"I want to share my story and my voice."

Your *why* matters. Your *message* matters. Your *book* matters. *You* matter. How you market your book matters, too, especially if you want to make your author emPact.

I leverage the Author emPact Framework as my guide when I meet authors. It's where I start each and every time. It's where we'll begin.

But as important as your *why* is, understanding what success looks like to you is equally as meaningful.

---

emPowered Thoughts

***Why* do you want to write a book? Or *why* are you writing a book?**

Take a moment to not just reflect on these questions half-heartedly, but to do so with purpose. Because your *why* is your cornerstone. It will dictate your next step.

---

1. Publishing Perspectives, 5.26.11
2. Not to fret! In chapter 3 you'll get all the ins and outs of this framework.

CHAPTER 2
YOU DETERMINE YOUR DEFINITION OF SUCCESS

I always look forward to the New Year. There's something invigorating about a new planner, a fresh perspective and 365 days of opportunity. Even though there is only a day difference between December 31 and January 1, it feels like a massive life change when the ball drops and the world gifts us with a new year to try to remember (or am I the only one who will still be using last year's date for the next three months on accident?!).

The New Year poses opportunities in a variety of ways. Fitness, for one, makes it onto many lists. (Myself included! I'm pretty proud that I got up and did yoga this morning. Check back in with me in a few weeks to see if I've kept up that resolution.) Success is also a goal for many. I spend days creating plans and laying out strategies to achieve them. While success looks and feels different for everyone—for some, it's monetary and others it's something else altogether—the push to do better, to be better and to make the year count is a goal we can all agree upon.

Some forms of success have clear measurements:

- If you want improve your fitness efforts, you may identify weight loss and how your clothes fit as metrics of success.

- If you want to grow your business, you may have key performance indicators to review monthly to see if your leads convert to clients, if your efficiencies impact your bottom line, and if your marketing strategies increase revenue.
- If you want to achieve a personal goal, you may outline key steps to accomplish that goal. For instance, if you have a goal to write a book this year, you may be able to measure that success by identifying how many words you want to write in a given time frame with an end date goal as progress toward that accomplishment.

Other success metrics aren't quite as straight forward:

- Improving your health may be your end goal, but success for you may not be quantifiable. Possibly success is increased energy as well as improved mood and overall feeling.
- Growing your business—to you—may mean more freedom and time which could equate to hiring more staff so you can accomplish more or tightening your team and simplifying your business.
- Writing a book may be your goal, but success may be less about the book itself and more about the emPact[1] that the book is going to make. You may not be a writer by trade and opt to have it ghostwritten (if that's the case, word count goals aren't your priority). Or possibly you have already written your book, but success for you is making the shift to writing a marketable book[2] and marketing it too!

SUCCESS IS SUBJECTIVE.

Don't believe me? Interview people you believe are successful and ask what success means to them. You will likely get as many different answers as the number of people you ask. I've been asking authors this question—"What does success look like to you?"—and I know first-hand that it's true for us too.

While knowing your *why* is the first place an author should start on their quest to make their author emPact, the second step on that journey is getting clarity on what success looks like. How will you know if your book is successful if you haven't determined what success for your book would be?

Simple question.
Complicated answer.

The truth is, only you can define that. But it's important to do, first and foremost, before you dive into:

- **Writing your book.** However, if you've already written and published your book, you still can still benefit from having clarity on success for you.
- **Publishing your book.** Because your book goals could—and should—dictate your publishing approach.
- **Marketing your book.** Since there are oodles of ways to market a book but not every tactic will align with your success metrics.

I'm happy to guide you on this journey by sharing ways I've helped authors uncover what success means to them.

ALWAYS START WITH THE END IN MIND.

For me, identifying what success could or should look like requires me to jump to the end. (This is telling about me as a person since I am one of those readers that reads the last page of a book before starting! Promise, author friend, not to hate me for this.)

I ask myself several questions:

- Where do I want my efforts to take me?
- When will I know that I've reached success?
- What metrics am I tracking to ensure I get there?

When I discuss goals with authors and how we will know we achieve them, I always start with their *why*. Knowing your *why* gives insight into what success will look like for you. There are many reasons—and *whys*—to become an author.

On a personal front:

- **Writing a book may be a bucket-list item for you.** It's something you've always wanted to accomplish, a dream you've never been able to shake. I helped a cookbook author to bring her dream to life and watching her joy in every step of the process brought me joy. She had high book sales because she was so passionate about her cookbook.
- **You have a message someone needs to hear.** Let me tell you, they *do* need to hear it! Your story matters and, in sharing it, you may inspire another person to share theirs too. I believe that books build bridges, not walls. In fact, they are powerful at breaking them down. Books give people a glimpse into the life of another in a way any other platform just can't. And your story could change a life. Now that's powerful!
- **You want to leave a legacy.** Your book—and your story—has the opportunity to outlive you. It can change the lives of people you will never meet. I've watched my grandfather publish a book about his life experiences because he wanted to leave a legacy. Knowing my children will know him long after his life here is concluded warms my heart.

On a professional front:

- **A book can help you make money.** The book itself can bring in income (I dare not say passive income because every dollar made from a book is a hard earned one). But a book can do even more. It can help you form a business. Actually, whether you mean to form a business or not, the moment you publish a book you become an authorpreneur. It also can inspire derivative offerings such as speaking engagements, workshops, workbooks and more.

- **A book can position you as a thought leader.** No longer are you just the person who said it; now you are the person who wrote the book about it. You may be a thought leader already, but having a book to support you and your message has weight. People notice. It elevates you and what you want to tell the world.
- **A book can help you start or grow a business.** The emPower PR Group is living proof of that! A book can become a business card for additional business opportunities. It can give you a tool to market yourself and your business. It opens doors for people to better understand how and why to work with you. And it increases your credibility and visibility.

Before you can identify what your book's success will look like and, in turn, how book marketing can support that, you need clarity on your *why*. It will help ensure that you are writing the best book to accomplish your personal or professional mission and identify the success metrics to make it happen.

Success, what does that mean anyway? Unfortunately, it's not like leggings; it isn't a one-size-fits-all. Success comes in a variety of shapes and sizes, thank goodness!

- Some authors equate success with the number of books sold or amount of royalties made.
- Others see success as emPact made, the reach of their message and the power of their message to change lives.
- Many see success as leveraging the book as a calling card for something bigger—a budding business, perhaps.

Success—while having a standard definition—can only be defined by the person seeking it. As you consider where you want to be a year from now, months from now, even a week from now, consider this question. *What will success look like for you?* Your answer is a gateway to identifying your marketing goals and success metrics that accompany them.

GOALS. ISN'T THAT JUST A BUZZWORD?

Quite possibly, but since I've been methodical and intentional about setting goals, something crazy has happened. I achieve them! Just like you would set exercise goals or nutrition goals… goals to get out of debt and goals to grow your family, your business or you career… just like you would strategize over any other goal in life, you should be just as diligent in setting goals for your success as an author. I encourage authors to articulate their goals early in our collaborative process. In fact, it's the foundation of our work together.

How in the world can I support a book's marketing efforts without knowing which approaches align best with an author's goals? Pro Tip: if a book marketing company is willing to sell you on a marketing tactic without aligning it with your book's goals, run and fast!

You don't need a slew of goals. One to three goals for your book is the perfect amount to start with. Your book's goals will—and should—inform your marketing strategies and success metrics.

Let's say that you have a goal of selling five hundred books a quarter. That's a lofty goal, but like I mentioned earlier, without a goal, how will you be able to achieve it? With that goal in mind, I would encourage you to focus on what movement *can* be done to help accomplish it. You can't strong-arm people into buying your book (bummer, right?), but there are metrics you can put into place to help you make incremental movement.

For instance, you could:

- Identify three companies a week that could benefit from your book's message and reach out about offering a bulk discount for them to purchase and share with their employees.
- Create meaningful tools to inspire leadership groups, masterminds and book clubs to leverage your book for deeper learning.
- Work with fabulous marketing teams like ours to identify a marketing strategy to get your book's message in front of the

right target audiences through social media, inbound marketing, micro media outreach, book marketing platforms or earned media.

Notice how the metrics inspire movement and can turn a lofty goal into tangible action steps to achieve it. That's how we roll at the emPower PR Group, and it's honestly one of our favorite things to help authors with.[3]

People are enamored with books—reading them and writing them. Even in the digital age and a world with fewer bookstores, I don't see books ever going away, thank goodness. If writing a book is something you've always wanted to do, then do it! If your book deserves more success than it has achieved to date, then make it happen.

Stop making excuses and take action. But before you do, ensure that you make movement with strategy in mind. Understand your *why* and gain clarity on your book and marketing goals. Then, clearly articulate what success will look like and create actionable steps to achieve it.

Writing a book can change lives. I've seen it happen for others. I'm proof of it too. It can and will happen for you too.

---

emPowered Thoughts

What will book success look like to you? Don't ask around. No one else can answer this question. And no answer is wrong. It's not a multiple choice question. There is no true or false. And I'm not grading this. Be honest with yourself.

If you have a tough time articulating your answer, here are a few additional questions that may help:

How do you plan to use your book? Sometimes this is a good indicator of what success will look like for you.

How will you know that you achieved your success? Is it a feeling? Is it a tangible goal?

Once you have clarity on the vision of your success, make it measurable. Outline three goals for your book that are measurable and the metrics that you will use to track them. Be kind with yourself and be realistic.

---

1. EmPact is the heart and soul of this book, can you tell?!
2. There is a difference between a book and a marketable one. While you'll dig into this topic in part 2, let me give you a quick definition. A marketable book is one that inspires action from its readers and it is one that is easily able to be marketed to your target readers.
3. I've captured some additional ideas and sample goals and metrics in episode 3.1 of *The emPowered Author Podcast*.

CHAPTER 3
GUARDRAILS AND ROAD MARKS

One Christmas, Santa gifted our children verbs instead of nouns. (Thank heavens Santa knew that the excitement of ripping wrapping paper was more joyous for our children than diving into the boxes of toys that they contained. I, inevitably, would find myself reselling many on online yard sales a few months later.)

Someone wise once told me to be in the business of collecting verbs not nouns—experiences over things—and I wrote Santa my own Christmas letter that year in hopes he would give our family this meaningful gift. And he did.

Three experiences awaited us. An overnight stay in a nearby castle—Kentucky has one that is a bed and breakfast—was on the list. A trip to Nashville, Tennessee's Opryland hotel was next up, complete with moments of speechlessness while walking through an indoor forest of plants and flowers from around the world and day-long laughs as we plunged into their indoor water park. The last, however, was my most memorable experience that year, and it wasn't for the best of reasons.

A trip to Gatlinburg, Tennessee, completed our Christmas gifts of verbs. I had been there before. I loved the simplicity of staying in the mountains, walking along the strip while meandering in and out of tchotchke stores and eating our weight in greasy delectables. It was bound to be amazing. And I trusted that Santa knew what he was doing when he secured our cabin nestled in the mountains. I was confident he took into account the need for simplicity and paired it with my fear of heights.

Surely he wouldn't forget the latter.

The promotional pictures of the cabin made it appear to rest comfortably on flat land, but the moment our GPS directed us off of the main drag and onto a one-and-a-half lane road for eight more miles until we would reach our destination, I knew I was doomed. I parked the car and told my husband it was his turn to drive before we traversed up the mountain. I am always the driver, so for me to surrender that title meant business, but I knew we were destined for twists and turns and drop-offs.

And I was right.

Every inch we made felt like a decade. My hands were sweaty, and my face took on the color of our maroon minivan. I closed my eyes as tightly as I could, but closed eyes on a windy road isn't a recipe for reprieve for this gal hates heights *and* gets motion sick. Occasionally, I had to bite the bullet and look out the window to calm my queasy stomach.

Ever felt like your breath was left behind you somewhere, in a place you couldn't find again? I did as we navigated up the highest mountain that I had ever been on. Thanks, Santa.

THANK HEAVENS FOR THE GUARDRAILS.

Focus was the only way I was going to make it to the cabin without a panic attack, so I began to focus on what I was grateful for instead of what was lacking. I could have put energy into the missing pieces of the road and the plentiful potholes that would create jolts of worry in the pit of my stomach each time we hit them. Instead, I found gratitude in the guardrails. They weren't stationed at every drop-off, but when they were, I felt a small sense of relief. At least we couldn't accidentally roll off the edge. The guardrail would save us! (Yes, I realize that is not completely accurate, but I took solace in anything I could find.)

Those guardrails became my best friends, holding me together when I was falling apart. They were my hope when I begged to be let out of the van so I could walk up the rest of the six miles alone and safe. They gave us enough restriction to guide our direction but also enough flexibility to navigate around a forthcoming car. (Gulp, those moments were terrifying!)

Who knew that a guardrail would mean so much?

WE ALL NEED GUARDRAILS.

A preacher once put into perspective the power of guardrails. They are pivotal, he noted, to direction and accomplishment while providing flexibility for detours when needed.

He was right.

- The guardrail was directional, helping us navigate the mountainous terrain without falling to our demise.
- The guardrail was the source of our accomplishment, helping us reach our end destination of the most amazing cabin on the tip top of the Great Smoky Mountains.
- And the guardrail had flexibility, allowing for detours for others who were nestled within the forest instead of the mountain top. It also gave us the confidence we needed when we had to inch closer and closer to the edge to pass another vehicle.

Guardrails give us hope, confidence and direction. The preacher used the analogy to speak to one's faith, but I saw even more extensions. Literally, I had just experienced it. But, figuratively, I realized it is how I tackle book marketing.

THE AUTHOR EMPACT FRAMEWORK IS AN AUTHOR'S GUARDRAIL.

I had countless sleepless nights contemplating an author and how we were marketing his book. I couldn't figure out why our current approach wasn't yielding better results. Things weren't adding up. And as someone who also debated being a math major in college, when something doesn't add up, I can't sleep until it does.

We had followed the approach I had utilized time and time again with other authors, and I knew the book marketing strategies and tactics I had identified would work. They were effective. They made sense. They would help him sell books. But they weren't working for him.

During a strategy call, I decided to go back to the basics. I opted to ask a simple question, one that is now the *first* we ask all authors.

Why did you write this book?

Quickly I followed by asking him: *What would book success look like to you?*

His answers prove that not all book marketing strategies are created equal. I had expected his overarching goal would be what I thought most authors' overarching goal was: to sell books. Why would you write a book if you didn't want to sell it?

But that wasn't his goal. In fact, he couldn't have cared less if he sold any books. He was more than happy to give his books away as he saw them as a business tool. The number of books he sold didn't matter to him. He was focused on how many lives were impacted.

That day I had an epiphany. **Not all book marketing strategies and tactics have relevance for every author.** Unintentionally, I had been trying to fit a square peg in a round hole. I thought there was one way from point A to point B. But I was totally and completely wrong. There are multiple paths to reach your destination, you just need a guardrail to keep you on track.

I stepped back and evaluated this author's *why* and what he needed to get there. The outcome was simple but purposeful. It was directional but flexible. It focused on a goal, but wasn't the goal itself.

That was the beginning of what I now call the Author emPact Framework. This framework is a tool used at the emPower PR Group to ensure book marketing strategies align with an author's *why*. Ready for the guardrails? To become an emPowered author and to make your author emPact, there are three concepts to consider:

- **Ensure you write a marketable book.** There is a difference between writing a book and writing a marketable one.[1] A marketable one will trigger word-of-mouth promotion and continue to market itself. A marketable book will help build or grow a business.
- **Selling books may be pivotal to creating your author emPact.** While this is what most authors see as success, it's not a part of every author's goals. But for those who have a message to share and want to build a revenue stream doing so, this is important.[2]
- **A book can be a tool to build or grow a business, and that may be your primary goal in publishing it.** Knowing that, your marketing strategies and tactics may be less focused on the book itself and more focused on how that book helps with your business goals.[3]

The Author emPact Framework highlights that emPowerment comes when these focused efforts collide because, in reality, you can't do one without the other.

If you want to sell more books, **you have to write a book first.**

If you want to grow a business leveraging a book, **you have to write one and utilize it in your business.**

If you want to write a book, **you will likely want to either sell that book or use it to align with a business effort or both.**

Each of the circles within the Framework have merit independently, but magic happens when they collide. While each seems very straightforward to the naked eye, as with any iceberg, it's just the tip of much, much more.

"Thanks, Stephanie, for this Framework, but I have a very important follow-up question," you may be saying. *"Where do I start, and how is this my guardrail?"*

I see far too many "deer in the headlights" looks. Literally, since my family lives on a farm in rural Kentucky, deer are always venturing into the streets. And figuratively, I see this when authors come to me wanting to write or market their books and haven't a clue where to begin.

I am not fond of this look. The eyes glazed over. The invisible *poof* of brain overwhelm the moment they realize this writing, publishing and marketing a book thing isn't for the faint-hearted. There is nervousness and concern for making a wrong move. Let me start by saying this.

Your path is unique to you. And only you.

While you may make a mistake, it can likely be fixed. While you may take an unexpected detour, you are always welcome back to the main highway. And it is going to be okay. I promise.

You are doing something massive and important. It's scary. You want to do it right. But there isn't *one* right. There are lots of ways to accomplish your goal. And as long as you are moving up the mountain, you will reach the top.

The Author emPact Framework is a guardrail for where to put your marketing energy. See it as a guide to help you achieve your *why*. Don't become immobilized by it. Let it make you free.

REMEMBER WHY YOU WANTED TO WRITE A BOOK IN THE FIRST PLACE.

Your *why* will never steer you astray. It is your best guide because it will let you know when you've accomplished it. Reflect back on the *why* you uncovered in chapter 1. Write it on a note. Stick it on your book, on your bathroom mirror, on your desk—anywhere you may find your mind wandering. It can ground you, and it can be your marketing answer.

While there are typically three categories of author *whys* (to share a message, make an emPact or generate revenue), you may question if you can have multiple *whys*. Sure. Anything is possible. But I believe at your core you have one that is the leader of the pack. What is your *one*?

The three parts of the Author emPact Framework overlap purposefully. Where they intersect, you will see a *why* highlighted. Knowing your *why* lets you know where to begin.

- **Want to share a message?** If a book is the conduit you feel called to share your message through, the way to do so is by writing a marketable book and selling more of them.
- **Want to make an emPact?** A book can do that, and so can a business. Writing a marketable book and using it to build or grow a business may be your North Star.
- **Want to generate revenue?** A book and a niched business can make that happen! (While you need a book to do that, the focus is on selling books and building or growing your business alongside.)

Knowing your *why* helps focus your energy on which marketing strategies to tackle whether you are investing your own time or seeking a team to support you.

If you want to share a message and make an emPact, please don't neglect the importance of writing a marketable book. It will be worth every penny in the long run. Nothing pains me more than to meet with or work with an author who didn't consider how to make their book marketable in the first place. (If that's you, deep breaths! You can still market your book. I promise.)

If you want to share a message and make money doing so, selling books matters. Of course, writing a marketable book and building or growing a business at the same time will help, but at the core, you could focus your energy on book sales and reap the benefits.

If you want to make a lasting emPact, writing a marketable book and building or growing a business alongside is the perfect pairing. And, if I'm being honest with you, most authors I get to collaborate with live in this sweet spot.

FOCUSED MARKETING TACTICS YIELD THE HIGHEST RESULTS.

My dad worked in the trucking industry for decades. He helped truck drivers navigate their routes across the country. His goal was two-fold: a safe and timely delivery for the truck driver and for his customer's products.

He worked in the industry before cell phones were a thing. He navigated country roads before GPS existed. He had to determine how to reroute his team when a detour was inevitable without having an app to propose the next best path. He knows his stuff. And he also frustrates me to the core when he gives me directions.

"Alright, Steph. Here's how you get there. Go up a ways until you see the tree that is jutting out into the road. Turn right and you'll follow that road up over a few hills and round three turns, I think, until you see that run-down house that has way too many things in its yard. Just about a hundred feet after that, take another right, and if the wind is blowing thirty degrees north, you'll get where you are wanting to go in no time."

Thanks, Dad. (Behind the scenes I put the address in my GPS and let Alexa give me directions.) In all honesty, though, Dad's directions are sound. He knows because he's been there, and he identifies road marks to guide him.

I guess I get more from my dad than eyes as deep and rich as chocolate and a humor as dry as a California red wine. I see the road marks of book marketing through the same lens. Your *why* will help prioritize your focus. And your focus will uncover marketing road marks.

The subsequent chapters dig into each of these road marks for you, but for now, let's look at them from a bird's-eye view.

- **If you want to write a marketable book, you need to know your audience intimately and write to them.** And, while you are doing so, you will want and need to create a content marketing strategy to draw them to you while building your author platform. If you are wondering when the right time is to market your book, it's now, when you are writing it.
- **If you want to sell more books, you need to ensure that your target audience knows about your book and trusts that it is a solution for them.** You will want to launch your book and build a visibility and engagement strategy to reach your target reader. You will also want to go where your readers are by leveraging partnerships.
- **If you want to build or grow a business alongside your book, you will want to ensure you have marketing strategies in place that align with your offerings.** And you will want to ensure that you can actually sell what your business hopes to sell.

The following parts of the book are dedicated to the three sections of the Framework, offering you tangible ways—guardrails and road marks—to tackle the effort you have in front of you.

GUARDRAILS ARE ONLY POWERFUL IF YOU USE THEM.

When we were at the bottom of the Smoky Mountains, eight miles from our cabin, a very large piece of me nearly opted to get a hotel at the base and allow my family to navigate up to insanity alone. But I knew that tackling this fear would mean I would be gifted memories I'd cherish forever.

I would have missed my kids' first hot-tub experience. I would have missed the wonder in their eyes as they looked out across the mountain tops with a confidence that they could conquer anything. I would have missed movie nights together, complete with popcorn and family cuddles.

I would have missed a lot. And I didn't want to.

You may be feeling a bit like I did at the bottom of that mountain. It's safer where you are now, not taking action to fulfill this need to bring your message to life and/or share it with others. But let me tell you that isn't safe; that's selfish.

If you feel called to share a message, I believe you have to.
If you feel called to write a book, I think you need to.
If you feel called to build a business, I think you must.

It's scary, for sure. It's nerve-wracking, I know. But it's worth it. And one day you'll savor how a kernel of an idea pops into that delicious movie-theater buttered popcorn you can savor.

Guardrails provide you guidance to stay on track, but they are only useful if you are willing to navigate up the mountain. And to do so requires you to take the first step.

———

emPowered Thoughts

Where does your journey begin? Do you need to write a marketable book? Are you ready to sell your book? Are you wanting to build and grow a business from your book's messages? Your *why* will be your guide.

What could hold you back? We all have fears. Knowing them is the best way to overcome them. Are you scared of sharing your story? Are you worried about what others will think? Do you feel like you aren't good enough or worthy? These are reasons I see firsthand from authors with impressive credentials (and I share that with you because behind every façade is a person who has fears too). The best way to push through them is to call them out and let them know you have plans to move past. You can and you will.

What guardrails do you need and want? While the rest of this book provides more guardrails than were present on my trip up the Smoky Mountains, take some time to reflect on guardrails you may need. Are they people? Are they processes? Are they tools? Do you even know yet? Knowing them will help you wave your white flag of surrender and ask for help when you need it most.

---

1. In part 2, we will discuss how to write a marketable book—a book that isn't just written for you; it's written for your reader!
2. In part 3, we will discuss how to position your book for success and ways to keep momentum in book sales beyond launch.
3. Whether you know it or not, the moment you publish a book you are building a business. Part 4 of this book is an authorpreneur's dream.

CHAPTER 4
CREATE A RIPPLE

In my humble book marketer opinion, the most successful authors don't sell a million copies of their books (I mean, they could!) but, instead, they create a ripple.

We all know what happens when you throw a rock into water. The rock pulls a portion of the water's surface down with it while it sinks, but the water doesn't sink. It quickly rushes back to the surface and lets the rest of the water's surface know what just happened. And, in doing so, it creates a ripple. We may see the beginning of the ripple but don't know where it ends. It creates a pulse along the surface much farther than any eye can see.

Ripples extend reach. And authors can leverage that ripple to make their author emPact.

"IF YOU SAY IT MORE THAN ONCE, WRITE IT DOWN."

That was advice I was once given, and it's really sound wisdom I like to share too. If you find yourself sharing insights, thoughts, advice or tips multiple times, it's likely worthy of jotting down so that you'll remember it for later. And so that you can share it with others in a meaningful way too. Like through a book!

I am an expressive person; I like to use my hands to help communicate my thoughts. Probably too much! While working with authors, I kept finding myself explaining how to make the greatest emPact and largest reach in the same way. With my hands.

I would always start with a circle first, connecting my two hands to make as close to a perfect one as possible. Then I'd explain how that circle could extend out, with a pulse pattern like a ripple in water. Each ripple was purposeful. Each built momentum.

After discussing this process a few times, I realized it was time to write it down. The Author emPact Method was finally visualized and articulated.

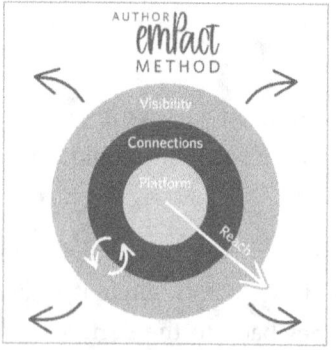

Much like the Framework, the Method provides a guardrail to success. It lets us know where to start first, where to go next and where to complete our efforts. It's methodical—obviously!—but it's flexible, allowing each author to embrace their interests and those of their readers as they achieve their goals. This Method can help you do that too.

The Author emPact Framework helps you prioritize your roadmap; the Author emPact Method helps you make it happen.

A RIPPLE CAN'T HAPPEN WITHOUT THE ROCK.

The rock is your foundation. It's the starting place. For authors, the rock is equivalent to the author's platform.[1]

An author platform isn't as flashy as the last part of the Method: Visibility. Many authors want to jump right to the end, thinking the more they spread the word about their books, the more their books will sell. Those authors may have limited and concentrated success, but they won't likely have long-term momentum. And, I don't know about you, but I'd much prefer longevity.

If you want to create a ripple, you have to start with the rock. You have to begin with your author platform. This is how people learn more about you, your book and how to take action from it. Your platform is consistent. It's your home. It should feel like you and speak your language. It should allow your readers and potential readers/clients to decide if you are a good fit for them.

After a marketable book is written and ready to be published (or while that book is in the drafting phase), our team pivots to the Author emPact Method for direction. And we start with the author platform.

THE FIRST RIPPLE IS ALWAYS THE BIGGEST.

I couldn't skip a rock if my life depended upon it, but ripples… I can make those! And when it comes to helping authors be emPactful, I'm in the business of making ripples.

The first ripple is always the biggest. It has to be, it's what creates the momentum that makes the other ripples possible. The first ripple in the Author emPact Method is Connection.[2] It isn't a flashy part of marketing. But it is the most meaningful.

There is a group of people—whether you know it or not—who love you, believe in you, want you to succeed but aren't quite sure how to properly support you. **These are your connections.** Your connections are your warm leads who, when emPowered, can help you create and keep momentum. And, guess what, they *want* to! All you have to do is tell them.

These connections become your army of message sharers. They start telling people about you, your book and your message. Before you know it, you will start seeing book sales even when you aren't doing anything to make those happen. It's because your street team is! And, if you have a marketable book, that street team extends to become much larger than you could ever imagine.

IT'S EASIER TO CONVERT A WARM LEAD THAN A COLD ONE.

The last ripple—Visibility—focuses on leveraging other people's platforms to convert potential interest into readers, clients and more. This ripple can feel safer because you don't have to be vulnerable with the people you know; instead, you are vulnerable with people you don't know yet.

There is a time and a place for a visibility strategy,[3] but it shouldn't be the first place you go.

- What would happen if you had amazing media coverage for your book without a website to tell people how to buy it? *Probably fewer book sales.*
- What would happen if you guest blogged on another website but didn't have a place to recommend potential readers to go to learn more about you and your business? *Likely interested clients questioning if you mean business.*
- What would happen if you pitched yourself for paid speaking engagements but the meeting planner can't dig into your thought leadership online? *I'm pretty sure they would pick a different speaker.*

Once your platform is rock solid (pun totally intended), and your connections are equipped to help spread the word, a visibility strategy is extremely effective in bringing in new connections and new possibilities.

Part 2 of this book will fully embrace the Author emPact Method, but I didn't want to wait until then to plant this seed. I wanted you to know the importance of the less flashy marketing efforts that pave the way for the shiny ones to be successful.

This is where the ripple continues. Where you will extend your reach. Where momentum begins. This is where you will make the greatest emPact.

emPowered Thoughts

Is your author platform rock solid? If not, you are in great company. Most authors have potential here, but it's important to note nothing is set in stone. You can create, build or build upon your author platform right now.

Take a moment to do what we call a digital presence audit of your author brand.[4] If someone searched your name and/or your book title today, what would they find? Would their findings help you achieve your emPact?

What marketing ideas do you currently have or have you already tried? Capture them, and tuck them away somewhere you can find. They are likely the shiny marketing approaches that are fantastic when implemented correctly. You'll want (and need) to start with your rock first.

---

1. Chapter 11 is all about author platforms, and it will give you more than you knew you needed to know to build or create yours.
2. Chapter 13 discusses how the emPower PR Group helps authors leverage their connections to extend their reach.
3. We will dive into how to build one in chapter 15.
4. Or reach out to us as we'd love to do that for you too.

CHAPTER 5
DON'T LOOK UP, LOOK DOWN

Years ago, I was approached by someone who had watched my journey as I moved from a seemingly comfortable and consistent job to an entrepreneurial life filled with lots of unknowns with a simple but game-changing question. He saw me build a business to fund my book writing and publishing process, publish and launch my first book, and build a new business to help authors do the same.

"Stephanie," he asked. "If you knew what it would have taken for you to get where you are now, would you have still done it?"

My answer was surprising. I love where I've landed, but if you want to know the truth to a question, ask someone at a time when they are trying to keep their three young kids from breaking everything they touch in a store full of breakables and they will answer with utter truth, even if they didn't know that truth beforehand.

NO.

No, if I would have known how much hard work it would take to start my own business, I wouldn't have even tried.

No, if I had known that for me to write a book I would have to go through a strenuous and vulnerable editing process, I would have bowed out.

No, if I had known that it would take starting a wreath business to help gain the confidence and funds I needed to write and publish my book, I would have opted for a different direction in life.

No, if I knew how hard it would be to accomplish what I have done, I likely would never have taken the first step to do it.

But there are two sides to *no*.

No, I can't imagine having not written a book and the freedom that writing provides me now.

No, I can't imagine a life without the ability to inspire and emPower others.

No, I can't imagine not having the chance to work with such varied authors and businesses across the world to help them bring their messages to those who need it most.

No, I just can't imagine what life would have been like now if I had known the hardships and not taken the first step anyway.

Surely I'm not alone. Reflect on your life with me for a moment:

- If you would have known how hard it would be to raise children, would you have been open to growing your family?
- If you would have known how hard it is to train for a marathon, would you have ever taken the first lap?
- If you would have known how challenging it would be to manage staff, would you have ever dreamed of being a leader?
- If you would have known how hard it is to write a book (and then market it), would you have ever typed the first word?

Most times, if we knew what we know now, we wouldn't have gotten here. On a podcast interview once, I shared an analogy I've come to realize is my truth. (And you are welcome to adopt it, too, as yours.)

I'VE ALWAYS IMAGINED MY GOALS AS A MOUNTAIN PEAK.

The snow-covered beauty is high up, where the air is thinner and the ground is uneven. The goal sits there, where only the most dedicated ever reach.

Oh, what I would give to make it to the top of Mount Everest to see the beauty from that view. (Just don't make me drive up it. Guardrails... I *need* you!) But have you ever considered what it takes for professional hikers to make that trek? More than I'm willing to give.

People say, "Keep your eyes on the prize." I say, "Keep your eyes on your feet." If you want to scale the mountain to meet your final destination, there is only one thing you can do: move. Take steps. Keep walking in the direction of your goal. Don't worry about the obstacles along your journey. When you meet that hurdle, you will figure out a way around it. Don't worry about the moments when your feet get stuck in mud. The mud will dry up and then you will be able to move yet again.

Instead, look a few feet in front of you... right where your next step will land. Keep your eyes on your feet. Focus on the steps you take. For when you do, you will one day look up and realize that you have reached that peak that once looked totally and completely unreachable.

And, if you are anything like me, you may also make another discovery. You may find that the mountain of a goal you had was never a single mountain. Instead, your goals are a part of a full mountain chain that, at one time, felt so far out of reach. But, by the time you've accomplished one, you will have learned that if you keep your eyes on your feet, you are more likely to reach your end goal destination.

Trekking to the top of one mountain was a feat, but you did it. And you'll see that anything is truly possible.

WHAT IS YOUR NEXT STEP IN YOUR BOOK MARKETING JOURNEY?

The answer is more simple than you think.
Movement.

You have reflected on your *why*. My hope is that you are holding on to it like my kids cling to me—with such fierceness that they will never let you go.

You have gained clarity on what success looks like to you. Fantastic! Jot it down. Then put it in a drawer that you can visit whenever you want to, but that you don't see daily. You don't have to see the sun rise each morning to know it will happen. You believe it. And you rest in that belief.

You know your goals and success metrics, but you don't have to look at them daily. Schedule time to evaluate them regularly, but give yourself room to make movement before you do.

Movement is your next right step. And movement doesn't require future visioning; it requires purposeful action. Today. Right now.

THIS BOOK IS YOUR GUIDE FOR MOVEMENT.

There are many ways that you can leverage the marketing goodness poured into these pages, and only you can decide what works best for you, your book and your book marketing needs. But let me suggest a few options for consideration.

1. **Be one of those beginning-to-end readers.** No matter where you are on your journey, you will likely find insights that will help you. Some of the best knowledge comes when you least expect it. If you have time, energy and a commitment to not let book marketing overwhelm you, read this book cover to cover. You will be glad you did!
2. **Choose your own adventure based on your *why*.** By now you know how pivotal your *why* is. Start there! If you've not yet

written a book, dive into part 2 and learn how to write a marketable one. Then you can pause, complete the manuscript and move into part 3. If your book is already out but you want to sell more copies of it, start with part 3 and get marketing insights on how to sell more books. If you have a business and want to leverage your book to build or grow it, start with part 4. You won't be disappointed.

3. **Use this book as a reference guide.** This book can be your guide for future efforts. Maybe your first book is already published but you totally and completely want to ensure your next one is a marketable one. Come back to this book when you are ready. If you want to sell more books but you don't have the time or financial investment to make that happen, no sweat. You can breathe life into your books whenever you are ready. If you want to build or grow a business, but Life is a bit complicated right now. It's all good. You can one day, and when that day comes, this book will be here for you. Waiting and ready. I hope you see this book as a resource for you wherever you are and whenever you need it.

READY FOR THE JOURNEY?

Had I known how many twists and turns my journey to the peak would entail I would have likely stopped. Don't let the mountain peak be daunting. Don't let book marketing as a whole stop you from trying something. Instead, focus on what is within your span of control—right here and right now—and make a promise to yourself each day to just keep moving.

Onward and upward.

---

emPowered Thoughts

What do you have capacity for right now? Take inventory of your current capacity—mentally, physically, financially—and let that guide how you use this book. There is no right or wrong way. The "right way" is the way that is right for you. And, remember, movement of some sort is all we are going for.

Where should you start? Honestly, if you ask me, my answer is anywhere. As long as you start, I'll be happy. Book marketing can be overwhelming, I know. I hear it day in and day out. So, start small. Start focused. Just start.

PART TWO
WRITE A MARKETABLE BOOK

marketable book (n): a book that speaks to and inspires readers to take action, and highlights how a reader can lift the learning from the page into their own lives

CHAPTER 6
DO YOU *NEED* THE BROWNIES?

I probably shouldn't admit this, but my most profound marketing insight came in one of the most peculiar and unexpected of circumstances.

I always knew that while I went to school for communications and marketing, my most important learning opportunities would happen outside of the classroom. I just didn't realize it would happen inside of a grocery store during my first shopping trip as a newlywed. Yes, in the middle of the snacks aisle, I had a marketing *aha* moment that changed how I look at everything. Seriously. No joke. (You can't make this stuff up!)

Let me invite you in on my life a few years prior to that moment. Upon graduating college, I was ready to experience the world and jump into my career. I was close to a freshly printed diploma, and it felt like all the opportunities awaited. But, after a few job interviews, I found that my pie-in-the-sky dream was available but at a cost.

I secured a job. *Amazing.* But the salary was horrific, especially for a gal who was living on her own with a cat to feed.

I sat down with my dad, who always seems to know the right answers to any of my financial questions, and learned about a budget. It was a depressing conversation, really, since my newly accepted job paid me barely enough to cover my monthly expenses and nothing more. But I walked away with a focused budget, outlining exactly what I could spend to ensure that I could still pay my mortgage. There was no wiggle room for extras. If I wanted to stay above water, following the budget was the only way to do it.

Each month, I had to stay regimented to that budget, which was neatly outlined in a college-ruled notebook. It ran like clockwork.

Pay the mortgage: *check.*
Pay the utilities: *check.*
Cover my gas to work: *check.*
Pray I didn't need a doctor's visit unexpectedly: *check.*

My measly paycheck dwindled quickly, but each dollar was accounted for since each budget line item was tight to begin with. Living on such a strict budget was challenging, but the hardest line item to abide by was the food category. This gal likes her food, and after sifting through all of my fixed expenses, I was left with seventy dollars for the food budget.

Yes, you read that right, seventy dollars. That's it.

If I overspent, it would have to come from another budget line item, and honestly, I didn't have the flexibility for that to happen.

Before you question how I made it through those years without dwindling to nothingness, it's important to note a few things for context. I am a vegetarian, so there was no meat required within that budget. And this was eons before organic foods were a priority or gluten-free options existed. I lived on boxed processed meals for years, and I stayed within my budget. Somehow, someway I made it work. I *had* to make it work.

THAT IS, UNTIL MY FIRST GROCERY SHOPPING TRIP WITH MY HUSBAND.

We had just returned from our honeymoon in Jamaica—all tanned and ready to begin our new life together—but we needed food to stock the fridge, so we went grocery shopping. I pushed the cart through the aisles rather quickly, focusing on the items I knew we needed and trying to not be swayed to purchase something I typically wouldn't. That was how I'd lived for so long on my own. But my husband was like a kid in a candy shop, so when he threw in a box of brownies I stopped dead in my tracks.

Brownies. *BROWNIES*. How do you say no to brownies? Nowadays, I don't! But you have to remember that back then I was still in my tight-budget mindset. I hadn't realized that two incomes to work from meant we had more flexibility in our grocery spending. I had been conditioned to be focused and purposeful, and brownies felt... well... like we were going rogue!

I stopped the cart, to his surprise (and mine), and picked up the box, asking him a question that now we laugh over.

"Cory," I began. "Brownies? Seriously? Is this a WANT or a NEED? Do you *need* the brownies?"

He looked at me like I had sprouted a new head and was probably questioning our recent nuptials. (In reflecting on this memory, I don't blame him!) I proceeded to reinforce that if it's a *need*, then that's a different story. But merely a *want*, well, that would require us to take something from another need. We had to be able to keep our shopping trip within our budget.

To my surprise, he said so matter-of-factly that brownies were very much a *need* in our household. They gave him a pick-me-up when a bad day ensues. To him, there was nothing like the deliciousness of the chocolate melting in your mouth right after pulling them out of the oven. And he reminded me that they were the perfect dessert for the two of us, because he preferred the gooey middle and I savored the crispy outer edges.

To Cory—my new husband—brownies were totally a *need*. I may have seen them as a want or a "nice-to-have," but as with most things in a marriage, it's important to give and take.[1]

HOW IS YOUR BOOK LIKE A BOX OF BROWNIES?

That day at the grocery, I had a "light bulb" moment. Several, actually.

First, I realized I needed to take a deep breath and chill out. The only way this marriage was going to be a happy one for the both of us would be if I learned the power of flexibility. Now, after adding three kids to our crew, it pains me to admit that I can't even look at the grocery bill anymore because it will give me heart palpitations.

But I also realized that much of our spending choices are like that simple ole grocery trip. And knowing that can make all the difference for authors.

You see, our world is built on *wants* and *needs* whether you realize it or not. Typically, when you think about what you are going to invest your income toward each month—how you will budget, per se—you likely think in these two buckets (even if that thinking is subconscious).

You have the *bucket of needs*, which typically is the first bucket you fill up. I'm talking about basic needs that you must have to get by. For most, it's things like food, shelter and clothing. For some, it includes the internet and a car payment. For others, their gym membership is a necessity. For me, vacations always make the needs list. Not everyone's needs are the same, but everyone does have a set of needs that, to them, are non-negotiable.

Then you have the *bucket of wants*; these are the "nice-to-haves." Dipping into this bucket every now and again is expected, but many times, this is the bucket that people will ponder before investing in:

- *Do I really need to go on that vacation?* For some, the answer to that is a resounding yes—so much so that it's really a need in their lives. For others, they may opt to do less frequent vacays.

- *Do I really need to purchase that outfit?* For some, that's an absolutely, and for others, it's a "maybe it can be a Christmas gift" kind of outfit.
- *Do I really need to snatch a copy of that book?* For avid readers like myself, I never question buying a book, but for others, it may have to be a topic that can really move the marble in their lives for them to justify it.

Understanding how your target reader needs your book is pivotal, but you can't determine that until you gain clarity on *who* your target reader is in the first place.

YOUR BOOK DOESN'T HAVE TO REACH SEVEN BILLION PEOPLE TO MAKE AN EMPACT.

I hate to break it to you, but it likely won't. And maybe it shouldn't.

It's common to answer the age-old question every marketer asks every author—*Who is your target reader?*—with the one-word answer: everyone. Secretly, I giggle when I get that answer from an author, not because I don't believe them but because I know the truth from it.

If you try to reach everyone, you will reach no one. It's depressing, I know. But it's reality. While you may think having all seven billion people in the world know you, love you and want to read your book, it's not critical to helping you make your author emPact. In fact, the varied wants and needs of all the people who populate this planet are immense. Trying to speak to each of them with your book, your message, your business and everything in between could make you feel like you are trying to juggle more than your two hands could keep up at once.

With that in mind, let me ask you again: Who is your target reader? Do you know? If you don't, that's okay! Most authors haven't a clue. The good news is that I have some questions to help you uncover them.

- **Who has told you to write a book?** This is a great place to start as it could be indicative of a target reader segment that doesn't just want your book, but *needs* it.
- **Who will benefit from your book's message?** Take a step back and reflect on who could be changed by the message you are sharing in the book's pages.
- **Who sees value in books and in books within your topic?** Your target reader may really need your book, but if they don't leverage reading as a tool for knowledge sharing, writing a book may not be the best approach to sharing your message.
- **What subsets of your community could be changed from your book?** Don't be afraid to go small. There is value in niching down, especially when it comes to books.
- **Who will invest their time reading it and their money buying it?** We are seeking two forms of investment from readers: the financial investment in purchasing a copy and the time investment in actually reading it. The most emPactful books don't sit on a shelf only to collect dust.

Once you identify a handful of target readers, go deeper in your research. This extra step will help you in more ways than writing a marketable book. It will help you identify how to market it:

- **Who are they?** Consider their demographic make-up such as their age, relationship status, family design, occupation, income, education level, primary language and life events.
- **What are their interests?** Do they have hobbies? Favorite publications or TV shows? What websites do they frequent? Do they have a unique shopping behavior? Are they loyalists to a specific company, group or organization?
- **What are their pain points?** What keeps them up at night? What holds them back from achieving their goals? What do they worry about? What would they benefit from knowing more about?
- **How can your message be their solution?** How can you help them most? How can your book solve their problem?

When you take a targeted approach to determine who your reader is, your book will be stronger and your book marketing efforts will be more effective. Take the time to do target reader research. Put yourself in the shoes of someone who would be interested in you, your book and your message. Only then will you be able to uncover how your book is a *need* that they don't know they have yet.

PIVOT YOUR BOOK FROM A NICE-TO-HAVE BEACH READ TO A MUST-HAVE *NEED* NOW. AND PRONTO.

Once you gain crystal clarity on your target readers, the next step is figuring out their *needs* and ensuring your book speaks to them. While they may still purchase your book if it's a *want* in their lives, know that they are **more** likely to add it to their Amazon shopping cart and click *buy now* without a second thought if your book is a need they can't live without.

Let me share an example.

When I wrote my first book, I knew it had the power to make a difference in the lives of many. And while I am grateful it did, I was worried initially because I began to hear responses from potential readers like:

"It's one of those that I pick up when I need a pick-me-up."
"What a great book for my next vacation read!"
"I can't wait to give a copy to my granddaughter for Christmas."

While lovely compliments, I found it as proof that some saw the book as a "nice-to-have" and not a "need-to-have." If I wanted it to make a difference in the lives of those who needed it most, I needed them to *need* the book, whether they knew they needed it or not.

I tried many unique marketing strategies, and most have been successful! (I wouldn't be writing this book if they hadn't.) However, there was one in particular that blew things out of the water.

I had a dear friend I kept feeling called to collaborate with. She was busy—and so was I—so it took a year after the book's release before we met up for soup and sandwiches to discuss ideas. As with any strong and effective strategic partnership, I knew we needed to have a win-win situation for the two of us.

I was an author with a book on mindset and perspective.
She was a nutritionist and virtual fitness coach.

Our messages intersected at a specific point for people. Both of us attracted people looking for balance and health in their lives. For her, that health need was physical. For me, the health need was mental. And yet, those who wanted to be successful with their physical health likely required mindset work, and those who were deep in mindset work likely realized the importance of inviting those approaches into how they care for their physical bodies too.

Together, we knew we could move mountains, so we decided to create a month-long offering where we focused on full body wellness—a body, mind and soul experience—where people could learn how to care for themselves from the inside out. Interestingly enough, while we didn't charge anyone to participate or require that they purchase a book or her fitness programs, it was one of my largest book sales months to date.

"Why?" you ask.

Because for people to eat right and exercise regularly, they have to have the right mindset to embrace the perspective I offered. For those who were motivated to care for their bodies already, they knew the importance of caring for their mental space. And for those who wanted to exercise and eat right but were having troubles doing so, they knew that they had to work through their mental barriers. I was a *need* for them, and so was my book.

IF YOU WANT TO BE RELEVANT, YOU HAVE TO MEET A NEED.

If you want to attract readers, you need to meet their needs.
If you want to sell your book, your book needs to meet their needs.

How does your book meet the needs of your target reader? How is it a solution to a problem that they are experiencing? How does your message alleviate a pain point of theirs? How does your book change the way they see the world, see their careers, see their lives?

When you focus on meeting a *need* rather than a *want*, then maybe, just maybe, you become that delicious box of brownies in their proverbial shopping cart—something they see as critical to their lives right that very moment.

---

emPowered Thoughts

Do you know who your target reader is? If not, now is the perfect time to clarify that. In fact, I would recommend you pause the book development process and determine your answer to that question, because that answer could change everything about your book—from its layout and design to its core message and theme.

How are you a solution to your target reader's problems? Everyone has a problem… or two or three. And the world is full of false promises to fix them. Your book doesn't have to be. It can change lives, literally, when it meets the needs of another. (And that's some powerful stuff, huh?!)

Do you need the brownies? Seriously?! I'm curious. Are you an inside gooey fudge brownie consumer or, like me, the crunchier the better? Brownies are totally and completely a need for my family now, and I'd love to know if they are for you too. Find me on social and let's celebrate brownies together.[2]

---

1. Didn't expect marriage advice in a book marketing book, did ya? I'm full of surprises!
2. While I'm on Facebook, Instagram and LinkedIn, I dabble on LinkedIn most. DM me! We've got fodder for a cool convo awaiting.

CHAPTER 7
IT'S NOT FOR YOU; IT'S FOR THEM

I'm constantly asked how to write a book (and I think even more people want to write a book than admit it or ask me the question). Ready for the secret? Here's the million dollar answer:

You write.

You can't have a book until you write one. (And if you opt to use a ghostwriter, you may have a welcomed detour to this accomplishment, but still someone has to write it!)

I've had the chance to work with many nonfiction authors in various stages of their book dreams. What I've come to find as the key differentiator between just any book and a book that changes lives and sells as well is this:

ANYONE CAN WRITE A BOOK FOR THEMSELVES; BUT THOSE WHO ARE SUCCESSFUL, WRITE THEIR BOOKS FOR OTHERS.

If there is one thing that I have noticed, both as an avid reader and as a book marketer, it's that what makes a book stand out is who it is written for. Seriously. This is game changing. I've had the pleasure of helping many authors bring the book in their minds to the page, and, when I do, I prepare them for what very few are ever told.

The first draft of your book is for you.
The second draft of your book is for your reader.

This is a tough pill to swallow, but if you want to write a marketable book, it's a non-negotiable. You have a message you want to share, and to effectively share it requires you to write a book the reader will find valuable. Many times, unfortunately, that isn't completely congruent with the first draft of your manuscript.

I had the opportunity to work closely with an author who was writing a story outlining immense trauma she went through as a child. The story was full of heartbreak—for her as she relived it to bring it to the page, and for the reader, who she invited into some of the most vulnerable moments of her life.

I was one of the first people to read her manuscript, and let me tell you, I don't take that for granted. What a pleasure it is to get a peek into the rawest form of a story. And what a worry it is to share productive feedback with an author about it. But that's my job. That's what I am called to do. And thanks to my upbringing in the heart of Kentucky, I am able to do so with southern hospitality. Bless my heart, that's for sure.

I remember reading her book and making it to page forty. The story was one the world needed to hear, but the depths of sexual abuse this author endured was more than I could bear. I became a puddle on the floor that morning at page forty. I couldn't go on. I didn't want to.

I believed in her message. I knew it was important. But I also knew that readers have a different tolerance for hardship. They sometimes choose to read a book for reasons other than why an author writes it. That, too, is okay. It doesn't diminish an author's purpose or negate a reader's reason. Both matter.

PUBLISHING A BOOK THAT READERS CHOOSE TO READ ISN'T EASY.

It takes thick skin and a healthy dose of humility. And this author had both.

I shared with her my challenge in finishing the book (which I did because she had asked me to). I acknowledged the depths of disgust I had after reading it (as I should have, what she endured no one ever should). I told her about how I felt like she would always be a part of me now (and I couldn't shake what I now know of her abuse). And I gifted her with an opportunity that started with a simple ask.

"Do you want to share your story or do you want to evoke change?"

Both could happen but to do so required a second draft. Every story matters, but a story that changes people, systems and more requires rolling up your sleeves and doing the hard work of making the shift from writing a book for you to writing a book for your reader. She chose the latter.

We spent hours together, restructuring the layout of the manuscript to give the reader some reprieve between the challenging chapters. We brought in glimpses of hope amidst moments of despair because her goal was to lead the reader to forgiveness, not leave them in the valley of darkness. She rewrote some, but most of the meat of draft two was there, it just required a little reworking. We both were proud of the shift that she took because draft two was remarkable.

Draft two exposed what sexual abuse could do and does to people. Draft two created a tool for others to use to decrease abuse of this type. Draft two was a guide from pain to forgiveness for any and everyone. Draft one was for her. Draft two was for her readers.

HAVE YOU WRITTEN DRAFT ONE? IF SO, ARE YOU READY FOR DRAFT TWO?

The Write to Your Reader Framework helps authors navigate draft two by stepping outside of themselves and stepping into the minds of those who *need* their book most.[1]

As you've navigated the insights in this book thus far, you have been preparing for this moment. Let me share how:

- When you understand your *why* and your goals, you realize that to accomplish them requires someone to invest in the book or its offerings.
- You can start to see why you don't want to let your ego get in the way. It's a no-brainer to make sure that you write a book that someone who needs it will love and will share with others. (That's the cheapest form of advertising!)
- It's pivotal to understand your target audience—that ideal reader of yours—and understand what your goals are. It's important at this stage of bringing your manuscript to life that you find a way to merge the two.

While I want you to write a book that you're proud of, I also want you to write a book that somebody will buy and read. The moral of the story? If you want to write a book that will sell, you need to write to your reader.

There are three steps that you need to consider as you write to your reader: the manuscript, the book and the action.

IF YOU WANT TO WRITE A BOOK THAT WILL SELL, YOU NEED TO WRITE A GOOD BOOK.

Seems intuitive, right?! Unfortunately it's not. Time and time again I uncover books that had such potential but missed the mark.[2] I get so excited about what a book can do, and I get so let down when I realize that it didn't accomplish it.

When you write a good book—one that gives value and is a solution to your target reader's pain points—the book will sell and readers will talk about it. Remember that momentum we were shooting for in chapter 4? It's possible when the book you wrote is one others can't put down and can't stop talking about.

You have a message. You have a goal. Your manuscript should connect the two. You can't have a book without the manuscript, but a manuscript that isn't meeting the needs of your target reader becomes a book that individuals aren't going to buy. (Cue the tear-jerking music.)

What makes a good book? Here are some things to consider:

- Strong writing draws your target reader into it. I've been told by my friends in the fiction space that you should "show not tell." How can you tell your story by painting a picture versus outlining a series of chronological events? Strong writing always wins and is the main reason I tell every aspiring author that professional editing is a must!
- The flow of the manuscript takes readers on the journey that they need to reach the final destination. Does your current manuscript do that? Or does it have areas for opportunity?
- A good book encapsulates your unique author's voice. Unfortunately, most stories aren't original. What makes your story unique is you! Don't forget to bring you to the page.
- Everything about your book is intentional—from the chapter outlines to the use of italics, from the book length to the tone found on the pages. Nothing is by chance; it's all important to ensuring your reader is inspired by it.

THE MANUSCRIPT SHARES A MESSAGE, BUT THE BOOK ITSELF INVITES YOUR READER IN.

Don't neglect the book itself as it is a major player in your book's success. I know… I know… we aren't supposed to judge a book by its cover, but we literally do. And books with low-quality covers usually don't get the reach their message likely deserves.

I am a book snob. I know it. My family knows it. For years I would only purchase hardcover books (that is until I wrote one myself and realized the practicality of a paperback). My favorite weekend pastime is relaxing in a bookstore, perusing the shelves. I find myself drawn to beautiful covers, and immediately before I read the first word, I take a whiff of the book's pages. (I'm not the only weird person who does that, right?)

For me, a book is an experience and I soak it up. The physical book is what creates that. As you consider how to write to your reader, don't overlook the power of the book itself. Here are some points to consider:

- What does your book need to look like and feel like so that your reader will find interest in and take action to purchase?
- What should the cover look like? Should it be artistic? Have your photo on the cover? (Pro-tip: Do some competitive research to see what the market will bear.)
- What size should the book be? Many nonfiction books are usually 6" x 9", but there's reasons to venture from that. When I write a workbook, I know my readers want to write in it, so I opt for 8.5" x 11". If you want your book to feel cozy, a pocket size may be more effective.
- Should you offer your book in hardback or paperback? eBook or audiobook? Or all of the above?
- What colors align with your message? What colors sell in your book's category? What vibe do you want your reader to have and how can your book's cover (and its colors) help make that happen?
- How much should you charge for your book? And, better question, how much will your target reader invest in it?

A MARKETABLE BOOK EVOKES ACTION.

This action can (and will) look different across genres, but action still remains a cornerstone of a marketable book. This action can be in the life of a reader or in the lives of others that the reader will learn about. My favorite action is how you want the reader to collaborate with *you* after they read the book's final page.

- Consider how your book may inspire personal action. How do you want your reader to take action in their personal life upon finishing your book?

- Is there a larger action that you want to happen? A bigger change the community or the world can do and your reader can be a part of it?
- How can your reader take action to connect with you? To work with you? To continue learning from you?

WHEN YOU WRITE TO YOUR READER, NOT ONLY WILL YOU WIN, BUT YOUR READER WILL WIN TOO.

When you leverage the Write to Your Reader Framework, you ensure your book will be one your potential readers will want, need and buy. You won't lose. You and your reader win. Together.

Finding a way to merge your *why* with your reader's *why* is ideal. *Why* did you write this book and *why* will they invest in reading it? A promise I make when working with an author is that when you give value, great things happen. A book is an avenue for giving. When you give, you get the gift of emPact back in return. That's probably the best gift an author can receive.

---

emPowered Thoughts

Have you made the pivot from draft one to draft two? Do you have time to do so? (Or better question, do you have time *not* to do so?) A book written for the reader will outdo one written for the author any day.

Are you up for doing the hard stuff? Writing a book is hard. Writing a marketable book written for the reader is harder but worth it.[3]

---

1. If you are interested in learning more, holler! It's a part of The emPowered Writer Program.
2. I probably haven't read yours yet, so I'm not talking about your book! Not yet anyway.
3. For more tips on how to write to your reader, listen to episode 3.3 of *The emPowered Author Podcast*.

CHAPTER 8
YOU ARE BIGGER THAN YOUR BOOK

When you are working on writing a marketable book, you may find yourself so deep in the weeds of the book's message—its words, its tone, its everything—that you forget something majorly important.

You, my author friend, are bigger than your book.

Yes, I realize you are literally bigger, but I mean it in a richer, figurative way too. Your book doesn't define you. It's not your worth. It may be a defining moment in your life that highlights a worthy and memorable event you've experienced, but the book in and of itself isn't either.

Why am I telling you this? And why now? Because a large part of writing a marketable book requires you to know this, embrace it and leverage it.

A MARKETABLE BOOK IS A CONDUIT TO SOMETHING MORE THAN THE BOOK ITSELF COULD EVER DO ALONE.

Your book may be a door opener for a business you have or a tool to build the business you've always dreamed of having. It may help capture your legacy so you can pass down your knowledge to others who need it. It may become a revenue stream that funds parts of your life you've never been able to afford or pour into a nonprofit you are passionate about. The book itself is a stepping stone to these things.

But you are bigger than your book. You are the link between it all. You are the glue holding the message and what happens next together.

There are a few words in the marketing world that some may think are of a different language altogether. Phrases like "lead magnet" and "nurture sequence" or words such as "opt-in" and "platform" leave authors' heads spinning. (Rest assured, my goal is to have as few heads spinning as possible.) As I strategize with authors, however, I realize that the word itself may not be unheard of. Instead, it's likely that the definition is too vague or downright confusing to someone who doesn't have a background in the industry. (And, if it makes you feel any better, there are even many in the marketing industry who don't quite understand them either.)

We will uncover lead magnets, nurture sequences, opt-ins, platforms and more shortly, but right now, there are two other words we need to tackle first. These words are ones many authors I work with tend to get confused on. It's a relatively simple word duo that has more depth than they consider, initially.

AUTHOR BRAND

At first pass, some authors are quick to raise their hand saying, "Ah, Stephanie! I have one. I have my book cover, and I've gone through the branding exercise for that and landed on something I love." Yay! That is big and definitely deserves celebration. But I follow-up with some context outlining how an author brand isn't a book or a book cover. And I leave them with the reminder that they are always and will forever be bigger than their book.

"Oh, right. I know! I actually already have a company logo so I'm happy to share that with you," some also say.

Another accomplishment to shout for joy on, but just because you have a logo doesn't mean you have a brand. And it *definitely* doesn't mean you have an author brand.

An author brand is a hard marketing concept to understand and here's why:

Your author brand is bigger than a book, it's even bigger than you and it's definitely bigger than a logo.

Most of us think in tangibles. A logo: *check*. A book cover: *check*. I must have my brand in place, right? Maybe, but maybe not. A brand—at its core—is so much more.

- A brand is what creates feelings and connections and drives individuals to purchase, engage with or take action from you. That is more than a logo. Much, much more.
- A brand is strategic, methodical and full of purpose. In fact, my favorite graphic designer reminds me regularly that she loves helping to articulate what happens in our minds.[1]
- Understanding how our minds work ensures brand creation can drive the actions you are seeing.
- A brand is, in essence, a **promise** to its customers of what they can expect from products and may include emotional as well as functional benefits.

A brand is powerful and an author brand is too.

WHY TALK ABOUT AUTHOR BRANDS WHEN WRITING A MARKETABLE BOOK?

The answer is simple: every author needs an author brand. Hands down. End of story. No questions about it. It's a must. And your author brand plays a role in your book.

Think of your author brand like you think of your story because it, too, tells an important tale. *Yours!* Even if your book is the spitting image of the story you want to share with the world, never forget you are the character within your book and you have more to share than a single book ever can. You are bigger than your book, and your author brand should be too.

In fact, if you don't have an author brand, I'd like for you to take a moment to reflect on these points and consider what it could and should be.

- Your author brand should start with your vision and goals. Then see how the book aligns within that instead of tackling your author brand the other way around. (Don't worry, you are not alone if you took the roundabout way instead of the straight shot from the get-go.)
- When it's time to market your book, you may or may not be marketing your author brand. It's dependent upon the opportunity and the listeners/readers/attendees to whom you are promoting in the first place. It's also dependent upon your goals for that promotion.
- Books are judged by their covers, and authors are judged by their brands. Use that to your benefit and ensure it tells the story you want it to tell.
- Always ask yourself, who are you trying to reach? How do you want them to feel? This is important in your overarching brand, and when done right, it will entice your ideal clients and readers and repel others.

Branding isn't easy to articulate alone. You are too close to you. You know what your goals are and you don't see the areas of opportunity easily. You know your own intentions and it's hard to ensure those are accurately articulated. You wouldn't edit your own book, right? (And if you said yes to this, let me give you some of the best book marketing advice out there! Don't! Hire a professional editor and it will increase your book's quality tremendously.)

YOUR AUTHOR BRAND AND YOUR BOOK BRAND CAN TOTALLY BE FRIENDS.

And they should! Because friends usually have mutual acquaintances, and you happen to be that connecting piece. The two brands can absolutely play nice in the sandbox and can go together like peas and carrots. But they really should be unique, standalone entities and here's why:

- What if you plan to write more than one book?
- What if you plan to write another book that has a different target reader from your first?
- What if you plan to do more with your message outside of the book such as speaking engagements, workshops, coaching and consulting?

Your book has a brand identity that speaks to its ideal readers, but that doesn't have to align and likely shouldn't be the same as your author brand. They can connect and even resemble each other—like siblings in a family may—but they are equally as independent, being provided the opportunity for growth on their own and together.

Before we go any further, let's get clear on what a book brand is. A book brand, much like an author brand, is meant to evoke a feeling and an action. It leverages colors, fonts, imagery and more to do that. It's bottled up on the book's pages, its cover and even the size of the book. A book's brand should align with the book's goals. It should help ensure the book's message reaches those who *need* it most. It should entice the *right* person to pick up the book and read it.

Both brands are important; they are just different. They can speak to different people, utilize different visual tools and generate different feelings. One is not better than the other; they both matter. Immensely.

You may be asking yourself...

HOW AND WHEN DO I INCLUDE MY AUTHOR BRAND IN MY BOOK?

Ah! The most important question of this topic, and yet we had to uncover what an author brand was and how it differs from the book's brand to be able to get to this point. Your book has the opportunity to be a tool to promote you. And you are bigger than your book! If you leverage the marketable elements of your book strategically, you can provide glimpses into your offerings and author brand in meaningful places within the manuscript.[2]

In addition, when you are promoting your book, you may or may not be promoting your author brand, too, depending upon the promotional opportunity and the needs of the audience. Let me share a few examples:

- I love podcast guesting, and depending upon the podcast I'm being interviewed on, I may solely talk about my book and the elements found within it. Or I may find myself talking about how my book has allowed me to inspire others to find perspective in their lives through my workshops, speaking engagements and more. In the former, my book brand and its core messaging takes the lead. In the latter, my author brand gets to shine.
- I have created a great working relationship with my local library system. I've participated in several series events they offer. In one, I was one of the speakers in a wellness momentum series. In another, I was a workshop leader in an author forum. In the first, my book brand was front and center as I shared tips on perspective found within my book. In the second, my author brand was in charge as I spoke about the publishing industry to other authors.
- I have had the opportunity to do countless speaking engagements as an author. During one, I was invited to be a meaningful part of a women's retreat. The entire retreat was branded with *Color Today Pretty* pinks and purples! My keynote and subsequent workshops were extensions of my book. While keynoting for the National Association of Women Business Owners (NAWBO) during their annual awards dinner, I leveraged the elements of my book to align with my goals as an author and spoke to the hearts of women about perspective. While a similar topic and connection to my book, I spoke as the thought leader who penned the book, not the other way around.

The main places I see the pivotal need for an author brand are when the author is creating a website, building out a content strategy, selecting a social media approach and developing authorpreneur offerings.[3] But it's important to understand your author brand as you draft your manuscript. Because you aren't just writing any book—you are writing a marketable one. And your marketable book can and should direct people to your author brand!

emPowered Thoughts

What are your goals as an author? What do you want your book to do for you and how is that a part of you? Do you see yourself as your book or your book as an extension of you?

Who are you trying to reach? With your book (ahem, your target reader)? With your author message (this is where your author brand takes shape)?

How do you want people to engage with you? Do you see your book as a gateway to more? Do you plan to have derivative offerings that extend your message?

These questions will help you begin to articulate what your author brand could look like and why it's so extremely important.

---

1. An entire season of *The emPowered Author Podcast* is on author brands. Dive into season 2 for countless insights and tips.
2. Chapter 9 dives into how your book can help market you, so be prepared to get tips on leveraging your author brand accordingly.
3. Parts 3 and 4 of this book will provide greater context on how to develop and execute each of these.

CHAPTER 9
THE DIFFERENCE BETWEEN A WRITER AND AN AUTHOR

"What do you want to be when you grow up?"

Such an *original* question to ask fifteen or so young ladies who were students at my high school alma mater, I know. But I really was interested, especially since I was the guest speaker for a creative writing class. I figured a few aspiring authors were in my midst.

I will always have an affinity for my high school, which was equipped with annoyingly stiff plaid uniform skirts and girls from every walk of life. It was there I learned the power of my audible voice, though it wasn't where I found my written one.[1] I was thrilled to potentially inspire this group of go-getters to uncover theirs.

I wasn't sure what I expected when I asked that question, but it wasn't yawns or silence. There was plenty of that, along with a handful who shared—surprising, right?!—that they wanted to be authors one day. That began our discussion on how what you want to be when you grow up may not be what you end up being.

I got giggles from the room as I shared that one of the first jobs I aspired to be was the grocery store bagger. I always liked the meticulousness of organizing. That was sure to be my dream job! Then it evolved into being a veterinarian, until I realized how you get a dog's temperature and that quickly became a no-go.

Writing a book, much less publishing it, wasn't in my plans. So the fact that these amazing ladies already had that as a priority in their life gave them a leg up in accomplishing it. They had written for their school paper and literary magazine too. In theory, they were also published. Such an amazing accomplishment, I truly believe, for anyone, especially a group of young ambitious women with voices that needed to be heard. And many of them had plans on writing novels, being journalists and becoming published. They knew I was already an author, but I was the one in awe of what the world would learn from these women when it was their time to share.

I dove into the thick of my presentation by asking my next question, one they weren't expecting. (I could tell because the silence was a bit longer than the "will the speaker just get on with it" type.)

"WHAT'S THE DIFFERENCE BETWEEN A WRITER AND AN AUTHOR?"

Crickets played their joyous tune in the fields that surrounded my high school as the ladies pondered what I had asked. "Not much," was probably what they were thinking, until one brave soul spoke up.

"Being published," she said with a mix of confidence and uncertainty.

She wasn't wrong. Not one bit. But, in my humble opinion, there is much, much more to the writer-to-author journey.

Before I wrote my first book, I didn't really understand—or even realize—there was a difference at all. But after being on the flip side of the publishing equation, the clarity is as clear as glass that writers and authors aren't one in the same. At least not at face-value.

From my point of view, here are a few of the differences I've noticed (in others and in myself):

- Writers focus on the craft of writing, while authors focus on the craft of emPact.

- Writers focus on the person doing the writing (the power of their perspective and their story), while authors focus on the person doing the reading (and how their story emPacts readers to take action).[2]
- Writers get excited about different goals such as word count, pages written, articles submitted, etc. And while authors love all of those too—also using them as a gauge of progress—they relish in the goals of leveraging a book as a door opener to something bigger, utilizing their book to change a life.
- Writers get jazzed about writing. Not all authors get jazzed about that, that's for certain! But authors do get jazzed about what the writing and their book can do—in their lives and in the lives of their readers.

Now, before we go any further, I need you to know I absolutely, one hundred percent, love, love, love writers and authors! Both speak my written language. But my goal as a book marketer is to help *authors* leave an emPact. And, for many, that may also mean they will sell books and build meaningful businesses from their messages.

Writers are those who write about the topic. Authors are the ones who publish a book about it. There is an unspoken difference there that deepens one's credibility and thought leadership. When you embrace the shift from writer to author—and when you decide to not just write any book but a marketable one—a big realization needs to happen in how *you* see *your* book.

It's a tool.

YOUR BOOK IS NOT ONLY A TOOL TO INSPIRE; IT'S A TOOL TO HELP YOU MARKET HOW YOU CAN HELP PEOPLE TAKE ACTION.

One of the first authors I supported opened my eyes to an unfortunately missed opportunity in the book writing space. Before I can help market a book, I have to read it. Yes, I realize this seems like common knowledge, but it's not the trend in my industry. However, it's how we can be most effective and best understand the author, their book and how the two collide.

I remember reading this book and letting out a big sigh. The book was beautiful—the cover was stellar, the content was butter and the message was poignant. The world was going to be changed by this book and this author. But my sigh was proof of a missed opportunity. A major target audience that would quickly embrace her message was one she had unexpectedly and unintentionally alienated in her book's content.

She was sharing her message, and her message needed to be heard. But she hadn't taken into account that a group who would be changed by her book—and would buy dozens and dozens of copies—may not have felt heard in the manuscript. It would be fine. There were lots of other marketing opportunities I uncovered. But that didn't mean I wasn't a bit timid to present her with the insights I had unearthed.

"Where were you when I was writing my book?" was her reply when I acknowledged some solutions to navigate around the touchy topic and still reach out to a major target audience in our marketing approach.

Great question. I had never considered how important marketing was in the beginning, middle and end of your book process. In fact, compartmentalizing book marketing for book sales misses the boat altogether.[3] Writing a marketable book—from the very beginning—and knowing who you want to emPact and how ensures that your book helps you accomplish your goals.

It is that simple.

The Write to Your Reader Framework helps you ensure that the meat of your book is written for your reader, but what about the potatoes?[4] What about the "extra" parts of the book that will help your book become that tool that inspires people to take action?

Well, let's uncover them.

TAKE ADVANTAGE OF EVERY MARKETABLE ELEMENT YOUR BOOK OFFERS.

Most authors focus merely on the book's character arcs, word choices, sentence structures and themes. All of those are important parts of writing a book someone will embrace. But, never forget, you are on the path toward authorship (and authorpreneurship too). There are countless other elements of the book that are usually overlooked, however they are full of marketing goodness—and marketable opportunities.[5]

Keywords

I know you've spent some time reflecting on your target reader. But have you considered how your target reader will search for a book like yours?

Keywords are individual words or phrases that your target reader is already searching for and, when used correctly, can help you sell your book. Knowing these words and phrases early in your book development process can help you integrate them into your book title, book description, publishing metadata and more.

Endorsements

Endorsements (otherwise known as testimonials) are advanced written praises for your book provided by someone who is influential and/or influences your book's target reader. Typically, their written praises are short, pithy, meaningful sentences that you can use on your cover, in your praise section and/or in your book's promotional efforts.

What I also love about endorsements is that they give you early feedback and support for your book and, when utilized correctly, they assist in building potential readers' confidence in the book prior to purchasing.

Book Title, Subtitle and Cover

First impressions matter, especially with books. In a sea of thousands to choose from, sometimes all a potential reader gets with your book is a split second to decide if it's worth picking up and reading. Your book's title, subtitle and cover have the power to create a meaningful first impression.

A few highlights worthy of noting:

- Your title should be catchy, and your subtitle should be clarifying.
- Unique is memorable, but ensure you are comfortable repeating it (and are able to remember it, yourself).[6]
- Remember to integrate keywords if appropriate and speak to a solution, not a reader's problem. (No one wants to buy more problems!)

Book Description

Congratulations! You have enticed a potential reader to pick up your book (or put it in their Amazon shopping cart) because you have an awesome cover and title. But before they open it and dive into its goodness, they will likely read the description on the back or the description online.

Don't let your book description be an afterthought. The title and subtitle pull readers in, but your book description hooks them.

Copyright Page

Depending on your publishing approach, you may have very little control over this page. However, if you do get a say-so in it, don't neglect that opportunity.

At the bottom of this page, you may be able to utilize it to assist in marketing you by adding a blurb about how readers can connect with you and how the book relates to other work you do they may be interested in knowing about and taking advantage of.

Dedication and Acknowledgements

Oh, the stress around which is what and where does each go?! Some authors use both in their book, and others don't use either. It's your choice, but if you want my humble—and very strong—opinion, here it goes.

Dedications are usually short and focused front book material that speaks to a few people individually or a group of people collectively that you want to dedicate your book to.

Acknowledgements are usually a litany of thanks found at the end of the book and provide you with a great opportunity to acknowledge specific people for their role in your book's development and your life as it pertains to your book.

What's Next?

No seriously, what's next? If you wrote a book your reader loves, they will want to know what's next. How can they work with you? What action should they now take? You can allow them to determine that on their own, or you can give them a nudge in a direction that is in alignment with where you think they should head.

About the Author

Your readers will want to know about you, and this section of your book gives you the chance to share as little or as much as you'd like and are comfortable with. Be sure to include a headshot[7] and a bit about yourself, your story and your credentials. This isn't a resume, though. This is a place for you to be real. People connect with people.

Connection

Your readers, whether you want them to or not, will likely want to connect with you. The question that matters most, in my opinion, is how do *you* want them to connect with you? This is a great place to share your website, social media platforms you engage on and email if you are down for receiving some fan mail!

Lead Magnet and Opt-In

I almost published my first book without adding this (so rest assured, even a marketer can forget these important pieces)! It's customary to want to build an email list so you can tell your readers about new books, offerings or more. And the best way to begin building that is by encouraging them to take action after reading and loving your book.

A lead magnet is what you use to get people to give their email address to you. It's your gift to them in exchange for their email. The opt-in is the process by which they receive the lead magnet. Let me share an example.

Let's say you wrote a book about leadership. Your lead magnet could be a top ten list on how to best engage with your team. The opt-in would be the signup form and email service that would allow your readers to provide their email and receive the top ten list as a gift back.[8]

SEE, THERE IS MORE TO A BOOK THAN YOU LIKELY THOUGHT...

… And so many marketing opportunities live within it.

The difference between a writer and an author really comes down to this: How are you going to use your book to help you spread your important message, make a difference in the lives of others and leave a lasting author emPact?

---

emPowered Thoughts

What did (or do) you want to be when you grow up? And, follow-up question, how did what you originally wanted to grow up to be shape where you've landed? Okay, now while this isn't important in writing a marketable book, it's a really fun question to ask yourself and reflect back on what you had considered being as a kid. (And this is a fun question to explore with your kids, your peers, your team and more.)

How can your book market *you*? Part 4 will discuss all things author-preneurship, but before you get there, I really want you to consider what you want your book to do for you too. Having clarity on what your book *can* do and what you want it *to* do will help you take full advantage of the marketable elements found within it.

What marketable elements do you need to embrace? Don't just *write* a dedication because you're supposed to. Use it! Don't just *collect* endorsements. Share them! Don't just *share* your credentials in your About the Author. Share you! What's next? *Decide* that and tell your readers that too.

---

1. I was more of a theater gal, myself back then. But I did fall in love with writing monologues, so there's that!
2. At least the most emPactful authors do, the ones who want to (and do) write a marketable book.
3. And I don't know about you, but if I'm on an island and the time nears for the cruise ship to depart, you betcha I'll be back on the boat early just so I won't get left behind.
4. I'm a vegetarian, but even before I set aside the meat, the side dishes were always the most delectable!
5. If you are interested in learning more about these additional marketing opportunities, visit the emPower PR Group's YouTube channel and enjoy the Write a Marketable Book playlist. Also, The emPowered Writer program is a focused journey for authors to help fully embrace all the marketable elements of a book.
6. There is literally nothing more embarrassing than forgetting your book's title and subtitle. Take it from someone who has!
7. I am passionate about authors getting professional photos taken for their books. From headshots to branding photos, I believe authors need to ensure their visual story aligns with their written one. (Okay, I'm stepping off my soapbox now.)
8. Want to see a lead magnet and opt-in live in person? Visit emPowerPRGroup.com and take advantage of ours (and get marketing insights in the process).

CHAPTER 10
DON'T JUST WRITE IT, PUBLISH IT

The main focus of my presentation to the high school creative writing class wasn't how to write a marketable book; it was how to publish one.

I asked them what they wanted to be when they grew up. They yawned. I asked them what the difference was between a writer and an author. They silently stared. But when I asked them what makes a book worthy of being published, they perked up. Ah, I had hit the question they wanted an answer to. (And it may be a question you, too, are contemplating.)

I HAVE GOOD NEWS, AND I HAVE BAD NEWS. WHICH DO YOU WANT TO HEAR FIRST?

My dad's famous question, and even if you pick, he has already decided the order in which he is going to tell you his enlightening thoughts. (And thank heavens, usually the bad news isn't so bad after all. That also means the good news isn't always good news, but you're in luck. Today it is!)

Let's start with the bad news.

If you aspire to write and publish a book, you may be swimming in a red ocean. *Blue Ocean Strategy* by W. Chan Kim and Renée Mauborgne is on my To Be Read (TBR) list.[1] So while I haven't yet fully absorbed this book's marketing insights, a friend once told me the gist.

You want to swim in the blue ocean. Where the water is crystal clear (and you can see the bottom). Where you can swim freely without worry. You don't want to swim in a red ocean. (Please don't make me pull out my fear of sharks to describe fully what makes it red.) In the simplest of descriptions, this is the ocean where you may not stick out and could possibly get gobbled up. Gulp.

The fact that you want to write a book puts you in a red ocean. (Deep breaths.) I mean, we're talking about two hundred million people who aspire to be published one day. That red ocean can be terrifying—immobilizing, actually—if you let it.[2]

Ready for the good news?

The shift to the blue ocean comes when you find your way to stick out among the crowd, the noise, the other books and authors out there. How do you do that?

Here's what I've figured out as an author life raft that much prefers the lazy rivers and blue oceans:

- *Quality writing*: While there are editors who can help you technically, there is a difference between quality sentences and quality writing. I'm talking character development, details that suck you in and a storyline that hooks you. Quality writing aligns with a quality story that *needs* to be told.
- *Unique voice*: How is your writing voice different from others? One simple thing: *you*. You—your voice—is your differentiator. And, once you perfect it, it could help you be the Adele in a sea of boy bands. (Alright, bad analogy, but you get the drift.)
- *Relevancy*: Every story matters. But when your story matters *and* relates to the world today, you have found that beautiful undercurrent that doesn't pull you out but helps you stick out.

- *Reader-centric*: A book written in your voice but with the reader front and center is a gold mine or, if we are keeping with the ocean analogy, maybe it's that beautiful sand dollar that you find hidden on the ocean floor.[3]

The calm waters and clear blue ocean for authors is found when your book encompasses your unique voice, is relevant in the market today, is quality writing and is reader-centric.

How do I get my book published?

If I were to sum up the number one question that I get asked the most, it's this one. (If you are wondering it yourself, nearly every other aspiring author out there is wondering it too.)

Before working in the industry, publishing was daunting to me. As it should be. You will likely only do it once or twice, maybe a handful of times in your life. Even if you perfect it the first time, you're likely to forget things the next go around.[4]

There are a lot of myths and unrealistic expectations about publishing a book. There are many unknowns, and that can cause aspiring authors a lot of worry. I'd love to break down these walls, pull back the curtain and share the pros and cons about the various publishing options.

MYTH 1: THERE IS ONLY ONE WAY TO PUBLISH YOUR BOOK.

Thank heavens this is not true because it allows so many more stories and messages to be shared. However, this is something many, many people believe—especially when they are aspiring to publish their first book.

You may only think of one solution to publish your book, but there are actually three ways to do so:

- Traditional publishing
- Self-publishing
- Collaborative or hybrid publishing

I'll share a bit more about each publishing approach, as well as the benefits and areas of caution for you to consider.

Traditional Publishing

Let's start with the publishing approach you likely think of first when you think of being published. Nine times out of ten, aspiring authors want to be traditionally published. They close their eyes and envision a publishing company twiddling their thumbs, awaiting their fantabulous manuscript. That publisher drops everything when the manuscript comes across their desk and picks up the phone to immediately secure a deal with the author that comes complete with a hefty advance and all the book promotion they could ever dream of.

I don't want to pop your dream bubble, but it would be wrong if I didn't. Traditional publishing is an amazing solution for some authors, but unfortunately the process to be considered and the process when you are selected doesn't work exactly like you think.

The definition of a traditional publisher is this: the publishing approach most authors dream of—finding a company that will pay them an advance for their work and take lead in publishing the book without any risk or investment on the author's end.

Sounds dreamy, huh? There are definite perks, but there are also some setbacks to consider before sending your manuscript to every traditional publishing house known to mankind.

Let's touch on the pros.

- *It sure does feel great to be chosen!* Most traditional publishers have very little capacity to take on new authors. They may only publish a handful of books a year, so if your book is selected, it just feels freaking awesome! We all like to be chosen.
- *Getting paid for your work upfront is gratifying.* While every traditional publisher is unique, some still offer an advance to authors, meaning that they will pay the author prior to the book's publication date for their work. Some traditional

publishers don't offer advances, but they don't require the author to invest in the publishing expenses either.
- *You can breathe and believe that your story is being pampered.* Traditional publishers have a team of experts on hand who know what they are doing and give your message and your book the mani, pedi and facial it deserves. Cue the cucumber slices.
- *You get more time to do what you love doing—writing.* Because you likely have a literary agent on hand to help you find a publisher and work with them, you can focus on your next book while this one is about to be birthed.
- *You can take advantage of the relationships that the publisher already has in place.* They may have a connection with a media outlet, bookstores, airport stores and more that help you get your message and your book a unique reach and visibility.

Every yin has a yang, including the dreamy traditional publishing approach.

- *Nothing in life is free.* Boo! But it's true. If you are being paid in advance for your manuscript, you are likely handing over your intellectual property rights and decisions you may want to make for your book. In theory, your publisher is buying your book and the rights to it.
- *Sorry, control-freaks but you likely don't get much control either.* Your publisher could make title decisions, cover design choices, pricing strategies and more without your weigh in, and you really can't fight that. This may not matter much to you, but if you want control, you likely won't have much of it with this approach.
- *An advance could mean less royalties.* Royalties are the payments authors get when books are purchased. If you get an advance, the contract usually has a stipulation in place where the royalties must hit a threshold before the author gets paid again. (And sometimes that threshold is never met.)

- *Being chosen also means that you are helping them too.* Never forget that publishing is a business. A publisher that chooses you likely has several criteria for doing so, and one may be that you have a large platform that will help them sell more books.
- *Tick, tock, tick, tock.* If your book is timely, let's hope it remains relevant. It could take quite some time to find a traditional publisher, and even more time for them to publish your book. You have very little, if any, control on the timeline.
- *A literary agent likely means you're sharing the payment.* Most traditional publishers require a literary agent to pitch a manuscript to them. And if the manuscript is selected, the literary agent will likely get in on the action.
- *Books don't market themselves, even if they are traditionally published.* Sigh. One of the biggest misconceptions out there. No matter how you publish, if you want to sell books, you'll have to market them.

Self-Publishing

On the other end of the publishing spectrum is self-publishing. Now, if you just did a cringe or felt a shiver go up your spine, have a chit chat with your internal self and put them in check. You just experienced the very unfair (but very unfortunately real) stigma that self-publishing gets. And while there are real reasons worth reflecting on, it's a new day, it's a new dawn, it's a new life and self-publishing can be really good too.

When most people outside the publishing world hear self-publishing, it likely is paired with low-quality. And I just hate that because I know some amazing self-published books that aren't in alignment with that statement whatsoever. (Though, I also know many that unfortunately are.)

The reason for this stigma comes at the root of what it means to self-publish and it's this: The author takes the lead on everything that both a traditional publisher and the author would do. This includes writing the book and all aspects of getting the book over the publishing hump including editing, proofreading, formatting, designing, uploading and promotions.

Now, before you have another head-spinning moment, I want you to hang on and see the great freedoms that self-publishing offers.

- *You get to do you.* And no one can stop you! If you have a specific vision of your book and what you want the book to do for you, self-publishing allows you to always hold the remote control. No one can come behind you and switch the channel. You are the keeper of it all. You get to dictate every step of this process. You get to choose the cover design and title. You get to choose how you want the book laid out and where it will be published.
- *You own it all and you get to swim in the gold as well.* I keep thinking of the DuckTales episode where Scrooge dives into his sea of gold. It's all his and when you self-publish, it's all yours too. You own your intellectual property and all of the derivative work you do that aligns. Plus, you get all the royalties from book sales.
- *You control your investment.* Self-publishing is the most cost-effective approach to publishing outside of securing a traditional publishing contract that offers an advance. In theory, outside of your time, you could publish a book at no cost. I cringe even writing that, though, because I do believe that there are several things you can't do alone—and never should—including cover design and editing. But, if cost is a worry of yours, self-publishing is an option worth considering.
- *You get to decide when your book is published.* The only thing standing between you and a published book is you writing it and uploading it. You choose everything—including when you will tell the world your book is ready for them to explore.

I don't know about you, but I can be my best friend or my own worst enemy. Same is true in self-publishing; there are so many perks and challenges yet, because you are in charge, you don't know (and won't know) until you know.

- *Ever published a book before?* The answer is likely nope, and that lack of knowledge may not work in your favor here. The publishing industry is nuanced and tricky. You can tackle it, but knowing who to go to for trusted advice isn't easy. You could, unfortunately, make some wrong turns in the process, resulting in your book not being the quality you hoped and not getting the visibility you expected.
- *Unfortunately your math teacher isn't going to average out this test for you.* The learning curve is large, and only you are there to learn it. You have to take the time to do so if you want to do it right, and this could turn into a large time-suck. If you don't have the time, that could be a major problem for you.
- *Quality and quantity is the perfect pairing.* However, because you call all the shots, there is a chance the quality of your book isn't as strong as it would be with a publisher. Because of that, some bookstores may not consider your book. Even if your book is amazing, there is a credibility issue in the field you will be missing.
- *And guess what, you have to do all the marketing for your book.* (And hint, that's true for all of the other publishing approaches, but I couldn't neglect it here!)

Collaborative or Hybrid Publishing

Traditional publishing is one end of the publishing spectrum, and self-publishing finds itself on the other. But in the middle is another—and newer—publishing approach that I find many authors opt for.[5]

Nestled neatly in the middle of the industry is a publishing option called collaborative or hybrid publishing. In essence, this approach has taken the best ingredients of self-publishing and traditional publishing and baked a new publishing cake from it, merging the two. Think of it as a confetti cake (my favorite), complete with baked-in sprinkles of various colors accounting for the parts of the other publishing options that were pulled in.

Imagine the deliciousness of all of your favorite desserts combined into one; that is what this publishing approach is like.

- *While every collaborative publisher is unique, most allow you to still own your work.* If ownership is something that is important to you, this approach usually allows for it—making it much easier to offer derivatives too.
- *You don't have to navigate the unknown alone.* You still have a team of amazing experts on hand to help bring your book to life. You can trust your publisher is giving your book the pampering you had hoped for and giving you some time to do some pampering yourself.
- *If you are risk-averse, rest assured that there is joint risk (and joint reward).* Traditional publishing puts all the risk on the publisher. Self-publishing puts all the risk on the author. Collaborative publishing allows for a joint risk and reward for the publisher and the author, which makes it a win-win for the team. While there are upfront costs for the author, they become a part of the publisher's family for a lifetime. Typically collaborative publishers offer higher royalties to the authors too.
- *You could have a book in your hands within six months to a year.* It may seem like a long timeline, but it's not at all! A quality book in the making takes time, and how awesome does it sound that you could be holding your story in your hands soon?

Ever heard the phrase *"If it's too good to be true, it's too good to be true"*? I remember thinking that too, when I learned of this publishing approach. There's always more to the story, and when it comes to collaborative/hybrid publishing, here are some things to consider.

- *The author usually has upfront costs, and they could be hefty.* In essence, the author is investing in the publishing team to bring the book to life. And there are so many moving pieces to the publishing puzzle to ensure it's done at the quality a book deserves. This publishing approach is usually the most expensive and impacts the author with the highest investment costs. Many see it as a pay-for-play experience.

- *You'll want to find a publisher that fits you.* Many publishers select their authors, much like a traditional publisher would. However, there are many publishing niches, and you will want to find the right publisher that fits your goals. It's hard to know who to trust in this industry, and that can be a bit nerve-wracking.
- *You can't dictate the timeline here, either.* You are at the mercy of your publisher and publishing team's schedule. That may work for you, but it may not.
- *And guess what is the constant here?* While your publisher may do some book marketing, you may have to pay for it. Marketing will forever be a responsibility of the author, no matter the publishing approach.

I can hear your deep sighs of concern as you read the publishing options and each of their pros and cons. I hear them every time I talk with aspiring authors about the publishing options. I know they are there because I experienced them. And then I rested in the truth that I would find a trusted author or two to guide me.[6]

MYTH 2: THERE IS A SINGLE RIGHT PUBLISHING OPTION FOR EVERY AUTHOR.

Not! I actually tell every single author that asks me about publishing that none of them are perfect. There isn't one amazing option. They all have benefits and pitfalls. While I am a glass-half-full kind of gal, authors see the realistic optimism in me in full force when talking about this topic because I know each option can be amazing for an author, and each will definitely present frustrations.

It's okay! The roadblock to progress is perfection. Don't seek perfection; seek the best right option. If you are debating what the best right option is for you, here are some points to consider:

- *Are you willing to invest in your publishing journey?* If you are, you may be more open to self-publishing or collaborative/hybrid publishing. If not, traditional publishing may be your best bet.

- *Are you wanting to publish your book by a specific day?* If so, self-publishing is probably the best option, especially if the date is near. If you have a date within the year in mind, collaborative/hybrid publishing may be worth exploring.
- *Go back to your why.* Why are you writing a book? If you are doing it because you just want to write books for a living, I'd suggest seeking out a traditional publisher. If it's because you want to build or grow a business, self-publishing or collaborative/hybrid publishing may work for you better.
- *Want to ensure you make the most money off royalties?* Self-publishing is probably your best bet as long as you ensure you are publishing a high-quality book.
- *Are you overwhelmed with all things publishing but want to still maintain control over your intellectual property?* I'd recommend a collaborative/hybrid publisher.

I could go on and on with recommendations here, but it's living proof that every author is unique and that dictates the best, right publishing option.

MYTH 3: I HAVE TO MOVE FORWARD WITH THE FIRST PUBLISHER WHO SAYS YES TO MY MANUSCRIPT.

That's a resounding no way! You don't *have* to do anything, including go with any publisher who says yes. If you opt for collaborative/hybrid publishing or traditional publishing, you want to ensure you find a publisher that works best for you.

Here are some questions to consider when interviewing and selecting a publisher.

- Do you jive with them personally and professionally?
- Do you like their publishing approach and book quality?
- Do you trust them and are confident in their work?
- Do they publish within your genre and niche?
- Do they communicate with you how you prefer to be communicated with?

- Do they understand your goals and timeline and have the ability to work within each?
- Do you understand everything that is included in their publishing package and does the investment make financial sense for you?

Only *you* can answer these questions.

MYTH 4: IF I SELF-PUBLISH, I HAVE TO DO IT ALONE.

This is also not true. More and more companies are being created that are, what is called in the industry, supported self-publishing companies. They have editors, formatters, designers, marketers and more to help self-publishing authors publish with greater quality and ease.

I love supported self-publishers for some authors, but I would like to throw caution to the wind here. These resources are pay-for-play services and require you to typically lead the process. If you don't have overarching knowledge of the industry, your goals and what you need to get there, you could find yourself investing in services you don't need.

Just be cautious, methodical and ask for guidance!

MYTH 5: I CAN'T AFFORD TO PUBLISH MY BOOK.

I had a brief moment when I opted to have my first book published where I heard inner Stephanie say this. And then I let go and let Life guide.[7] In doing so, I ended up finding a way to self-fund my book publishing journey through fundraising and the creation of my wreath business.

I am living proof that if there is a will, there is a way. If you have a book the world needs, make it happen.

THERE IS NO RIGHT OR WRONG OPTION.

The only wrong option is to choose to write an amazing book and not share it with others. (Though that's just my opinion.)

When it comes to publishing options, rest assured nothing has to be permanent. Be sure to read contracts and have clarity on how you could change things up if you need to. Choosing a publishing approach is a personal choice. And depending upon your goals and needs, it may vary from one author to another. As long as you come to the table with open eyes and ears and clarity on what you get and what you don't, you should be fine. However, be prepared to be in the process alongside your publishing team.

This is your book.
This is your message.
Trust your team and allow them to guide you to success.

---

emPowered Thoughts

How can your book float in a blue ocean? No red oceans for me! Nope. Nope. Nope. And I'm sure you don't want to hang out there either. What do you need to do to ensure that your book is publishable?

What are your publishing non-negotiables? Having clarity on this will help you identify which option makes the most sense for you. Remember, there isn't only one right way. All ways can be right and wrong for different reasons.

Who can I go to for guidance? Authors are such hospitable people. Do you know any you could schedule lunch with? I'm confident they would love to share ideas for you to consider and even virtual introductions. And if I can help, reach out![8]

1. *Blue Ocean Strategy: How to Create Uncontested Market Space and Make the Competition Irrelevant*, W. Chan Kim and Renée Mauborgne, Copyright 2015 by Harvard Business School Publishing Corporation
2. And I know because one year for vacation we went to New Smyrna Beach, Florida, and there were at least two shark attacks while we were there! Never again. Nope. Not this girl.
3. In retrospect, I'm not sure if it's the best family outing or not, but when I would frequent the beach as a kiddo, hunting for sand dollars was the adults' favorite!
4. Sounds like childbirth too… hhhmmm…
5. However, I also know many authors who both self-publish and traditionally publish!
6. You may think you don't know an author, but you do! Hi, my name is Stephanie, and I'm happy to be your guide.
7. And God too. My faith has played a huge role in my book journey.
8. Visit emPowerPRGroup.com to learn more.

PART THREE
SELL MORE BOOKS

book selling (v): marketing approaches that encourage current or potential readers to make two forms of investment—a financial investment to buy the book and a time investment to read it

CHAPTER 11
BUILDING AND LEVERAGING YOUR AUTHOR PLATFORM

I recently asked attendees of a workshop I was leading what they felt when they heard the word "marketing." As expected, they shared mixed feelings paired with flushed faces and worried expressions.

- "Marketing makes me feel like I'm on a hamster wheel. I keep going and going and going, putting in tons of energy but not making any movement."
- "Marketing is synonymous with overwhelm. I feel overwhelmed just hearing the word."
- "Marketing creates momentum, which is exciting, but I never know the next right step to take."
- "Marketing is something I have to do but not something I want to do."

I get it. Even as a marketer myself, I've felt many of the same feelings. I believe that's because every day there's a shiny new marketing object. If marketing is overwhelming before you learn of a new technique, you might become immobilized just at the sight of it.

ANOTHER REASON WE FEEL THIS WAY, I BELIEVE, IS BECAUSE WE THINK MARKETING IS JUST ICKY.

We authors didn't sign up to sell. We signed up to write! We don't want to push people to buy our books or feel like those annoying used car salesmen trying to make a dime. Nope, not us.

I believe that it doesn't have to be unpleasant. In fact, I believe that we think it's icky because we have been marketed to *when we didn't ask for it*. There is a difference between being pushy with marketing and sharing information about something people want. Both require marketing efforts. But one is annoying and one is valued.

Marketing doesn't have to be gross. It is actually extremely helpful. If we don't market, no one will know about us. Without marketing, people who would *love* your book and your message wouldn't know about it in the first place. Think of all the people who are missing out—think of all the books not sold, money you haven't made and people you haven't emPacted—if you don't tell others about it.

Marketing isn't about being pushy; it's about connecting with the people who want your stuff and telling them about it.

Think about something you get excited about as I tell you about three things I do.

- For several years I homeschooled my kids, and I would count down to Tuesdays where I would get a curriculum discount at my favorite homeschool curriculum store. I never wanted to miss those limited offer sales, so I would wait patiently by my email for the reminders.
- I am an avid fan of Lush—you know, the amazing store that makes bath bombs!—so when they have their annual sale, I want to know about it, especially since they never offer sales outside of the day after Christmas. You can bet I'll be there, and I want Lush to remind me!

- Amazon knows me as the girl that buys *all* the books, so when they send me "you may like these books" emails, I'm likely buying from them.

This is all marketing, but it's not icky because I want it. Your readers—or potential readers—will want that from you too.

There is a difference between, "I'm going to provide so many pop-ups on my website that people will leave before they even know what my books are about" and "I want to provide lots of value because I have a message that someone—actually lots of people—will be inspired by." My goal is for authors to market like the latter.

Out of the million ways that you could have shared a message, you opted for this one—writing a book. But writing the book is only half the battle. Making sure people find it, buy it and read it is the other half. That's where marketing—and your author platform—come in.

AUTHOR PLATFORM? I'VE HEARD OF IT, BUT I DON'T KNOW WHAT IT IS!

The dreaded two words that many authors have heard of but few know the definition. In fact, I also danced around its definition until I read *Your First 1000 Copies* by Tim Grahl.[1] His definition was so simple, and it reminded me that simple is usually always better.

An author platform is simply the means by which you sell books. It isn't your website or social media accounts, although both play a part. It's not your email list as a standalone, although that matters. It's not your speaking platform, although that does have the word in it and can help you sell books.

In its most simplistic definition, an author platform is the means by which you sell books. And that, in and of itself, is so freeing (and probably still a bit confusing)! It's also a reminder as to why I offer up a guardrail because there isn't only one way to do this.

I know this because how I began to build my platform was not at all in the traditional sense. Remember my unexpected wreath business?[2]

When I decided to write a book, I began in hiding until Life decided hiding just wasn't fun for anyone.

I began blogging after encouragement from a dear friend, and through a serendipitous series of events, I found a book coach who encouraged me to continue blogging. She also shared how much I should be saving up to engage in collaborative publishing and marketing. Cue the development of my wreath business. People could buy a wreath anywhere, but hundreds were coming to me instead. With every customer I shared my story. I told them about this book and how they were helping to pave the way and I asked if they wanted to stay in touch.

I was collecting funds for the book's publishing process. I was collecting emails for future correspondence. And, along the way, I was building my author platform without knowing it.

MY GOAL WAS TO SELL BOOKS. AND MY TACTIC BEGAN BY BUILDING CONNECTIONS.

Your website will do that. Your social media pages will help. Your email list will create connection. Your speaking platform—whether it's in person, virtual, podcast guesting or more—will give you visibility. But without realizing that your platform is more than each of those, you can't use the tactics strategically.

Here at the emPower PR Group, we have a handful of mantras. One of them is this: *We don't believe in movement without strategy.* I feel the same about developing your author platform.

So, how do you build an author platform?

The most effective way, in today's world, is through leveraging online marketing tactics to help develop a digital business hub, an opportunity for connection and engagement, a way for people to make sure you are a great fit for them and a visibility strategy to reach new audiences of people who will want to know about you.

Simply put: focus on building connections and begin by creating a digital presence that allows for it.

Long gone are the days where people would meander to a shopping center to spend hours finding the perfect *anything*. My family lives close to an outlet mall, and the last time we went up there to kill time, half of the stores were closed, and the selections were awful. Whether we like it or not, that's just not how people shop anymore—and it's definitely not how they engage.

If someone hears about you or your book, the first thing they will likely do is search for it online. What will they see when they do?[3] Where will they be directed? Will it be easy for them to learn about your message, your books and how to purchase them? My guess is that you have some room for improvements (and rest assured, every author does)!

It's time to pull back out the Author emPact Method and focus on the center circle: the rock. Remember, that's your platform. It's where we begin when we focus on helping extend your reach and achieve your goals. Whether you have created a platform or not, consider what should be included in one. Or if this is the first time you've given it any thought, here are a handful of steps to help you.

STEP 1: KNOW YOUR PLATFORM'S TARGET AUDIENCE.

Never start marketing movement without clarity in this area. However, keep in mind when it comes to your platform's target audience, it may be just a hair different from your book's target reader. That's because your target audience should include your target reader and those who can influence them.

For instance, my first book was written primarily for Christian women ages twenty to sixty. The beauty about target readers is that just because you have a target doesn't mean that other readers can't (and won't) find your book fascinating! I quickly realized my reach was much broader. However, when I worked on my author platform, I made sure I unapologetically spoke to their audience segment and others who influenced my target reader.

What do I mean by that? Well, people go to trusted sources for information. If you and your book can be highlighted by those trusted sources, there is the potential for something awesome to happen: greater reach and emPact! Influencers could be podcast hosts, media personalities, meeting planners, CEOs and leaders, for example. I ensured that my platform was a solution for both, which extended my reach.

As you reflect on your target audience, consider the following:

- What do they *need* and want?[4]
- How are you a *solution* to meet their needs?
- What about *your* message is important in their lives?

STEP 2: CREATE YOUR DIGITAL STOREFRONT.

Your digital presence is, unfortunately, more important than your physical one when it comes to book sales. Rest assured that I fully believe your physical presence is important too, but if you want to reach the many, you have to be poised to do so. Embrace it or not, we live in a virtual world that is getting more virtual by the minute. No amount of toddler temper tantrums is changing that.

Make sure you are there. You are visible. You are you and you are controlling the message being shared digitally about what you bring to the world through your book. As you reflect on what this means for you, I want you to ask yourself:

- How will your target readers know you exist?
- How do they know if you are the right fit for them?
- Where are you visible online?
- Where can your target readers engage with you?
- Where can influencers find you? And, better question, where can *they* direct people to learn more about you?

People will search for you, so don't leave them wondering. Give them a place to land. You don't have to be visible in all the places, just the right ones. In my opinion, a website is the first place to start.

The best marketing is done authentically, and I believe it can and should be done through leveraging an author website.[5]

- Think about one of your favorite stores. Do you visit their website to get updates?
- Think about your favorite author. Have you ever visited their website to learn of their next book?
- Think about your favorite [fill in the blank], and I bet that you happily skip to their website regularly to see what's up in their neck of the woods.

Guess what. That's marketing! And those are platforms at their finest. But that's value-based marketing too. That's authentic marketing. That's the kind of marketing you want, the kind where people come to find you and see what you have to offer. If you *don't* have a website, how in the world can they find you?! (Just sayin'.)

Out of all the options for creating a digital presence, your website allows you to own the message. Now, you will likely also want to leverage social media,[6] Amazon's author platform and more. While each is important, the truth is that those platforms could go kaput tomorrow and you'd lose everything and everyone you connected with.

Don't allow that to happen!

STEP 3: PROVIDE AN OPPORTUNITY FOR CONNECTION, ENGAGEMENT AND CONVERSATION.

I can remember sitting on the Berber carpet as my mom would get the computer ready. It felt like time was in slow motion as I waited patiently for our dial-up internet to connect. I must have had more patience than I do now, because even when that internet would crash in the middle of an AIM chat message, I could keep my cool. Not so much nowadays.

Back then, connecting with people virtually was so exciting when an email would ding its presence in my inbox. (Now I tend to dread the email abyss.) I would feel heart flutters when I would see someone thought I was cool enough to send a note. (Now, I am actively unsubscribing.) I thought email was amazing. (And guess what? It still is, no matter how you feel about it.)

The truth is, nothing has been developed that is quite as effective as email. Even though messages get stuck in spam at times and email can get you bogged down, it's still the single most effective tool for building relationships and connections.

You may laugh at that, questioning if I know my stuff. I assure you I do!

I remember where I was when 9/11 happened. I was in high school about to go to my journalism class where we sat plastered to the TV, watching the events unfold with terror, praying the whole time.

I remember where I was when the severity of the pandemic took root. I was in my home office having a small panic moment trying to figure out how to navigate the unknown with the known and making the decision that homeschooling was going to be a new normal for our family.

Both of those situations were catastrophic, life-changing, horrific circumstances. I should remember those moments; I will never be able to forget them.

I also remember the day Facebook and Instagram had an unexpected outage for about six hours. I was at a church, working with a local author on the book trailer for his forthcoming book's release. It was so peaceful in the hills of the city, watching our videographer fly a drone and observing a moment with the author and his grandson as they walked hand-in-hand down a walking path. I noticed the tranquility and quickly questioned it. Surely something must have been wrong with my phone as I had no notifications dinging annoyingly.

Nope. It wasn't my phone. It was merely a reminder that if we put all of our author platform eggs into the social media platform bucket, we will be let down. Facebook and Instagram were down for six hours that day. And it has become a constant reminder to me that social has a place, but it's not the only place you should be.

Your website should have, what we call in the industry, an "opt-in."

This is a way for people to "opt-in" to your email list. Pause for a minute and take a mental inventory of your own email. If it's anything like mine, you likely have too many email accounts to remember and too many emails to ever read. Knowing this will reaffirm and better help clarify the need for a "lead magnet."

If an "opt-in" is the way someone can choose to get on your email list —and provide you with an open gateway for conversations and connection—a "lead magnet" is the tool to entice them to give up that prime email real estate. Time is precious, and no one has time to read all of the email forced our way. That said, we will read the email we want.

A "lead magnet" is a "what's in it for me" value-add offer. What is something that your target audience just can't live without that you could provide them with for free? It could be a top ten list, a guidebook, a tool or a resource. If they want it badly enough, they will "opt-in," giving you their email address and the permission to stay connected to them in the future. This isn't icky if they want it! Email marketing is only icky if they never wanted to be on your list from the beginning.

Email systems can allow you to deliver the lead magnet, create an email nurture segmented sequence and remain in contact with them in the future. I realize that if you are new to marketing, this may be stressful for you. Never forget that simple always wins! Here are the simple steps to make this work for you:

- Identify a "what's in it for them" value-add offer that your target audience would love to have and create it.
- Sign up for an email service such as Mailchimp.[7]

- Promote the value-add offer on your website with a form to sign up to receive. This form should be linked to your email service. (Note: This cannot be connected to your Gmail, Outlook or any other email service due to data protection laws.)
- Create an automated email sequence with your email service to deliver your value-add lead magnet and any subsequent messages to build connection.

Once you have this in place, incorporate it into efforts you already have underway. This can include adding it into your email signature, your social media infrastructure, your speaking engagements and more.

STEP 4: LEVERAGE IN-BOUND MARKETING TO FIND "YOUR" PEOPLE.

You know what I love about inbound marketing efforts versus outbound marketing efforts? Inbound marketing efforts allow you to be you. Outbound marketing efforts push you to be what others want you to be.

Let me toss out a caveat before we go any further. Remember in part 2 that I share the best way to market your book is to write a marketable book. A marketable book is written for the reader, not for you. It's your draft two, not draft one.

Inbound marketing is a new term I learned about while reading Marcus Sheridan's book, *They Ask, You Answer*.[8] If you haven't read this book yet, add it to your TBR list and put it at the top. His book outlines how inbound marketing draws people to you versus going out searching for them. Through content creation and sharing, you give people value while allowing them the opportunity to determine if you are a good fit for them. Content can be a conduit to value and a catalyst for connection.

When discussing content, keep in mind that it is value you give through various streams including blogs, articles, podcasts, videos and more. It's information shared in a way that gives value first and draws people into you second.[9]

As you consider how this plays into your author platform, reflect on these questions.

- What does your target audience find of value that you offer?
- How can you share that value in a meaningful way and in a way that they will be seeking it?
- Can you create a content calendar for the year to help you stay focused? (If not, that's okay!)
- How often are you comfortable sharing content and how/where will you share it?
- What tool will you use to share it? Where will you post it? How often?
- What will you do with your content once you share it? Do you have ways to repurpose it?

Content ideas can be endless and should be unique to each author, but here are some thought starters to get your creative juices flowing.

- Share parts of the publishing process with your connections. They may have never written a book, but they likely think the book writing process is fascinating.
- Give insights into your characters, your key themes or thought leadership.
- Invite your connections into your life on a personal level and show how it helps shape your book, your business and everywhere in between.

The goal of your content should be to give value widely and allow people to self-select if you are a good fit for them. Then invite them to join your email list. How you do it is unique to your capacity, capabilities, interests and enjoyment.

STEP 5: LET'S GET VISIBLE.

Once your platform's systems and structures are in place, it's time to test them out and get visible. Part of a visibility strategy includes your inbound marketing approach and leveraging your connections.[10] The other part includes leveraging other people's platforms to help grow your own.[11]

While we will discuss this in more depth in the coming chapters, it is important to note a few of my favorite ways to increase visibility.

- Reach out to people who reach your target audience. Those influencers previously discussed are natural fits here.
- Reach out to complementary service providers. They are people who serve your target readers in other ways. Strategic partnerships are brilliant to consider.
- Leverage outreach opportunities that engage your potential readers most. Work smarter, not harder.
- Be willing to adapt your message to reach new audiences. You'll be surprised where you find potential readers when you do.

As it pertains to your author platform, you may want to consider:

- Having a media kit on your website to make it easy for influencers to see your offerings.
- Ensuring your website and social media infrastructure is sound and speaks the same message.
- Be prepared, and afterward, tell your audience about it.

STEP 6: EVALUATE AND REFLECT.

An author once told me that reflection is the beginning of learning, not the end. And that's true when it comes to building and leveraging your author platform. Take time to evaluate your book goals, your success metrics and see if your platform and visibility efforts are in alignment. Here are some points to consider as you reflect.

BUILDING AND LEVERAGING YOUR AUTHOR PLATFORM

- Are you selling books? It's the heart and soul of an author platform. Is it working for you?
- Are your efforts creating the outcomes you want? Have clarity on what you can control and see if your efforts are producing results.
- Are there opportunities you are uncovering that are worthy of exploring? Books are good at uncovering these things. Create the space to consider them.

Marketing isn't a sprint; it's a marathon. Your author platform can—and should—start now, whether you have written the book, have published it or are looking to relaunch it.

---

emPowered Thoughts

Do you need to shift your mindset on how you see marketing? If you think it's icky, give yourself time to find the authentic marketing out there. I think you'll have a hard time marketing yourself if you can't move past the icky feelings.

Do you have an author platform or is it time to build one? Every author needs one. So if you have one, awesome! What do you need to do to strengthen it? If you don't have one, congratulations! Today is the day you will begin, and this chapter should be a great starting place for you.

---

1. *Your First 1000 Copies: The Step-By-Step Guide to Marketing Your Book*, Tim Grahl, Copyright 2020 Story Grid Publishing, LLC
2. If not, read the earlier chapter, "Been There, Done That, and It's Time I Wrote a Book About It."
3. Have you ever "googled" your name or your book's title? If not, you should! It's always a fun rabbit hole.
4. If you need a dose of audience inspiration, read chapter 6.
5. Season 4 of *The emPowered Author Podcast* is all about author websites.
6. Check out chapter 12 for more insights on social media for authors.
7. While these services change regularly, Mailchimp has a decent free version that I think provides a good start for authors.

8. *They Ask, You Answer: A Revolutionary Approach to Inbound Sales, Content Marketing, and Today's Digital Consumer*, Marcus Sheridan, Copyright 2017, Published by John Wiley & Sons, Inc.
9. Check out the emPower PR Group's YouTube Channel for content strategy insights.
10. More to come in chapter 13.
11. Chapter 15 gives you the skinny on a visibility strategy.

CHAPTER 12
THE AUTHOR'S SOCIAL DILEMMA

When I started working in the marketing field, social media was a completely foreign concept for businesses.[1] Facebook had just launched, and the rest of the world was trying to figure out what it meant to "poke" another person on the platform and why anyone would care about learning what someone else was doing right that very moment. Businesses didn't have Facebook pages, much the less engage in newsfeeds and stories. They weren't even available to do so yet.

The organization I was working for was less concerned about how to *use* the platform and more concerned about how their *employees* were using it. It's a crazy notion to think of today, when social media is a critical player in how everyone consumes information, but as with most technological advances, some of us remember what it was like before. Oh, those prehistoric days!

I remember a staff member who I managed was much more interested in Facebook than many others, and I was constantly asked to observe their time investment in it, for fear that it was a distraction at work. The leadership team didn't care about building social media into their visibility structure, they were more worried about creating a culture within the confines of their control where social media was a faux pas.

They set parameters around engagement, especially while employees were at work, and they definitely didn't want anyone talking about upcoming events on the platforms either.

Much has changed since then.

Social media evolved from Facebook being the primary platform to new platforms testing the waters daily. Some platforms become wildly successful; others dissipate about as fast as they attempt to make a splash in the first place.

The platforms have morphed into a tool for business as well—not just a networking site for individuals. In fact, businesses are booming that help others understand the platforms, engage on them and even advertise on them! You used to be able to put your head in the sand and mock those who took photos merely to post on social; now, you can't go anywhere without seeing someone making a TikTok video, selfies are out of control and some businesses opt for a social presence over a website. (Pro-tip: Reread chapter 11 and promise me you won't choose the former.)

Remember that organization that didn't want their staff on Facebook? Well, now many businesses have an expectation that their staff maintain visibility and engagement with potential and current clients on a plethora of social media platforms. It's become the way to **spread the word**, to **garner visibility** and to **make meaningful connections** for organizations, business owners, authors and authorpreneurs.

What began as a seemingly harmless tool to rekindle long lost connections and share some photos has become a livelihood for many and the cornerstone of most marketing strategies for businesses and authors. Speaking of authors, most find themselves with quite a dilemma when it comes to social media.

WHICH PLATFORMS SHOULD YOU INVEST YOUR ENERGY ENGAGING ON?

Ah… not just any dilemma. It's the social dilemma.[2] There are many social dilemmas out there, but this one may take the cake for authors—and any business owner, to be honest.

Unfortunately, the answer to this dilemma isn't a cookie-cutter one and varies from person to person, business to business and author to author based on a multitude of factors such as:

- What is your interest on social media? Do you like being on it?
- Where are your target readers/clients? Where do they engage most?
- What are your marketing goals? Will social media help you achieve them?
- How are you monitoring success? What metrics will you be watching?

Even though there isn't a clear, definitive answer on which platforms you should be on or how many you should be engaging with, there are three insights I believe are critical to determining where you should have a social presence.

ENGAGING ON SOCIAL MEDIA WITHOUT A STRATEGY IS LIKE JUMPING INTO WATER WITHOUT A LIFE JACKET DESPITE NOT BEING ABLE TO SWIM.

I can swim, but, no matter how many lessons I take my kids to, I am always fearful when we get near water. Call it my mother's instinct—or me being a semi-helicopter mom—but that life jacket goes on, and quickly, before we get anywhere close to a body of water! The true story is my youngest son and I nearly drowned in about two feet of water in a creek in our backyard.

That was a day I'll never forget.

We had just bought a twenty-five-acre farm, and we were loving the simplicity of the country so much that we invited some friends out for a bonfire. Our house hadn't been built yet, but we loved nature, we loved hiking and we loved the creek. Nestled in the farthest part of our land is a hidden gem—a running creek that has more creek stone than it does water most days. We love hiking down to it with our water boots and a spirit of adventure. Anything is possible when you are deep in the woods where you trade in cell service for ticks.

It was cold, I remember. But that didn't stop my littlest from jumping on the rocks. He was adventurous, and our creek was like a treasure map. As fast as he hopped from place to place, the mood shifted from excitement to terror. I glanced over to find him rolling in the water like a log rolls down a swift river. He had slipped off a rock and was trying to get footing on the creek bed. I waited a couple of seconds to see if he would pop up and laugh at his unfortunate circumstance, but that second didn't come. He was unsuccessful. He was drowning.

I jumped in, no questions asked, and when I did, I realized why he wasn't able to stand up. The creek bed felt like quicksand, and moss-covered rocks sat right beneath the water's surface. Every time I tried to lift my baby, I found myself falling down again on top of him. I was trying to save him, but I was actually making matters worse.

I yelled for help; we had a slew of friends by the creek with us, thank goodness. One friend came into the shallow water and pulled us to safety. I was terrified of what I would see, and for years I would continue to replay those moments in my head. But that day we were lucky. After a few coughs, my littlest had nothing to worry about except the cold temperatures and, thank heavens, a friend let us borrow some of their children's clothes to rectify that.

Drowning is real. I've seen it. I've been there. And I want you to know that it can happen anywhere: in shallow water and in the deep abyss. It can happen out of the water too.

I've experienced it with work overwhelm or parenting exhaustion. I've felt like I was underwater because of stress or uncertainty. When it comes to social media, I see many authors feeling like they have no idea how to navigate these uncharted waters.

My answer to their worries is this: Start with a strategy. (Please put on a life jacket.)

As with everything in life—especially in authorpreneurship—you really must have a strategy to be most effective. So, ask yourself, why do you want to be on social media? What is your reasoning? Is someone telling you that you must be?

Knowing your purpose can help guide you to which platform is the best fit for your goals. Not all social media platforms are created equal. In fact, many have different goals themselves, so knowing your goals and aligning them with the platforms' goals may be a recipe for success.

Test the water first. (You don't ever have to take a full dive in.)

It's important to go where your target reader is. Do you know which platforms they engage on most? Do they skew to a younger demographic, or are they always searching for bite-sized information? Do they tend to engage more with visuals or are they drawn most to videos? Knowing this can influence your strategy and, therefore, guide you to the social media platforms you need to be present on.

Ask for help. (Just yell for it, and help will be there.)

Nothing in life is meant to be conquered alone. You aren't going to get a superhero social media cape if you figure it all out yourself. Help is just a phone call away. Ask for it.[3]

WHEN YOU ARE STARTING OUT, IT'S EASIER TO JUGGLE A FEW BALLS THAN MANY.

Not everyone will agree with me on this. But I believe it's overwhelmingly true and it impacts not just what you can accomplish, but how your target readers (and social media followers) perceive you. You can create accounts on all the social media platforms out there, but if you aren't engaging on them, it could actually do more harm than good.

I'm good at many things, but juggling just isn't one of them. I thought that was limited to the circus juggling acts, but I realize I'm not all that great at juggling life either. (Can I get an Amen?) In case you haven't come to grips about this reality either, let me share some life-altering (and business-altering) advice I've uncovered with you.

You can't do it all now; but you can do it all. I realize life is short! I want to do all the things, be in all the places, accomplish all the goals. Someone recently told me I can. (Awesome! Thanks for the permission.) Then followed it up with, "You can do it all, just not all at once." That is so true in all aspects of life, including social media visibility and engagement.

Balance isn't possible. Wait, what?! There are oodles of books out there claiming to help people find greater work-life balance, but the proof is in the banana pudding. Balance just isn't possible. Some days you will spend more hours with your computer as you peck out your manuscript; other days you will forget what that computer looks like as you hike in the woods, swim in the ocean or do a puzzle with your family. Social media makes balance even harder, so as you consider how you want it to help your book and your business, make sure to ask how you want it to play a role in your life as a whole. And remember it likes to shake up balance.

A little is better than a lot. Unless we are talking about Little Caesar's Crazy Bread. Then a whole bag for dinner is absolutely fine. Right? (Okay, I'm the only one who stress eats that.) Slow, methodical movement will always win over the cannonball dive in. Go slow. Try a platform out. Get comfortable. Then layer on like you do clothing in the fall.

Instead of trying to be visible everywhere, have purposeful visibility somewhere. Choose a few select and purposeful social media platforms to be on and create a meaningful strategic approach to each. Build your following on those platforms and engage with your current and potential readers in ways that will deepen their connection with you. Once you have a high level of comfortability on those platforms—knowing how to use them, how to engage best and how to manage your resources accordingly—then you can re-evaluate if you should add a new social media platform to the mix.

IT'S ALWAYS ABOUT THEM, BUT WHEN IT COMES TO SOCIAL MEDIA, IT'S ALSO ABOUT YOU.

That whole "put on your oxygen mask" reminder that flight attendants do every single flight has much more context in life than we give it credit for. Really!

I've seen it ring true as a parent—if I don't have self-care, the thread holding me together unravels much more quickly than it should. It's true in business—you can't give everything to everyone all the time. If you do, you'll realize you've left no margin for you.

Even though the second draft of your manuscript is the shift from you (author) to them (readers), if you hadn't experienced what you have up until this point, how could you write a book in the first place?

The same concept has relevance when it comes to your presence on social media. Before you dive all in (with a life jacket, of course), take inventory on the time and resources you are willing to devote to building your social media presence and engaging on the platforms accordingly.

- Are you planning to manage your social media engagement? If so, know that to be most effective you must be visible and being visible requires time.
- How much time are you willing to give daily, weekly and monthly to plan and execute accordingly?
- What role do you want social media to play in your overarching book marketing plans?

Rest assured there are people available to help you if you'd like.[4] Social media content strategists and digital business managers can help you create effective strategies and build out meaningful content. They can even post content for you. But it requires an investment, of course—a financial investment to build your team and a time investment to ensure that your social media presence is authentic and meaningful to you. How much are you willing to invest?

Social media provides you endless opportunities yet, continuously poses dilemmas. You can attempt to put your head in the sand and boycott presence on any and all platforms. Maybe that will work for you. You can try being everywhere, and I'd like to check in and see how your sanity is holding up. Or you can be methodical about where you are and why you are there. Don't let social media run your life; tell it who's boss and make it work for you. A dilemma is only a dilemma if you don't accept the challenge and raise the bar accordingly.[5] At that point, a dilemma becomes an opportunity.

---

emPowered Thoughts

How do you feel about social media? I work with many authors who despise it. And rightfully so. However, there is a place for social media in an author's platform, and the only way to embrace it is to understand your feelings toward it.

Do your readers (current or potential) engage on social media? If so, which ones? Start with the strategy first. Find out if they are on social in the first place (if not, then maybe you get a "get out of jail free" card). If so, start your visibility efforts there.

What help do you need? There are loads of resources online to learn about each social media platform (the emPower PR Group's YouTube channel and podcast is a great starting place). But also know that you don't have to figure this out alone. Take inventory of your time and resources and never forget to ask for help if you need (or want) it.

---

1. Yes, I realize this dates me.
2. If you haven't watched the 2020 documentary *The Social Dilemma*, put this book down and go do it. Now. You'll never look at social media the same.
3. I'm always here if you need me.
4. Remember, all you have to do is yell for help. There's so many social media experts in this world one of them will probably hear you.
5. Season 8 of *The emPowered Author Podcast* is all about social media. If you are interested in learning more about the most important social media platforms for authors, tune in.

CHAPTER 13
READY. SET. LAUNCH! (OR RELAUNCH!)

That mountain hike to the top of the writing-a-book goal isn't as simple as some think. You'll need to carve a walking stick along the way to help with balance, ask for directions a time or two and remember to look down, not up.[1]

Part of the trek is actually writing the book. But when you do that, unfortunately, you won't find yourself on the top of the mountain just yet. That beautiful, serene scenery awaits, but you won't be able to soak it in until you tackle the second part of this book writing business —getting your message into the hands of those who could benefit from it most.

Some authors have a meltdown just thinking about it, but I say, "Bring it on!" (Not the meltdowns, the challenge of reaching your target reader.)

While I have very little in common with the cheerleaders from the 2000 teen cheerleading flick,[2] as a book marketer, I realize I am a cheerleader in my own right. In fact, marketing has a lot of similarities to cheerleading. Marketing focuses on the overarching goals and the areas of opportunity and screams direction from the rooftops (and the sidelines). It can be flashy, much like those pom-poms my daughter's dance team used that felt like watching a strobe light on repeat. It became something I could not look away from, though, as they captured my attention (and gave me a headache, but that's beside the point). When marketing works best—and if it's uber strategic—it can build a strong pyramid of marketing tactics from just about anything and anywhere. And—probably my favorite similarity—it can generate excitement, focused energy and emPact quickly, much like a half-time show. That is where the launch comes in.

WHAT IS A BOOK LAUNCH, ANYWAY?

If you're a part of an author circle, you'll have heard the word launch tossed around a bit. Because there are varied meanings, I think it's smart to clarify early on what in the world I'm talking about when mentioning it. This next sentence is going to go against everything you believe, but trust me when I say this: *A book launch and a book release are not synonymous.* You may initially think so, but believe me, they aren't.

Your **book release** is the day your book is published. Depending upon your publishing approach, that could mean the day it goes live on Amazon. It could mean the day the book is up on IngramSpark. It could mean the day you are able to purchase your bulk author copies. Typically, however, this is not the day your book launches.

Instead, when discussing your **book launch**, I am referencing the day your book is being promoted to the masses. This is the day you begin sharing with others that the book is available for purchase and you provide them guidance on how to do that. Typically, this effort is methodical, layered with a soft or internal book launch to those who know you, love you, trust you and want to support you (ahem, your launch team[3]) and a hard or external launch to those who could benefit most from your book's message (positioning you to meet a need for your ideal reader).

You have some control over your book release date. You can ensure you have your book written, edited and formatted within a specific timeframe. You can collaborate with your publisher and editing team to meet a target release date. However, printing is fickle (and so is Amazon, remind me to tell you about the time I was ready to release a book three weeks before Amazon finally did, and no, I'm no longer bitter!).

However, you *have* total control over your book launch date. And, when done right, your book launch can be game-changing for you and your book's success. In fact, your book launch could:

- Help you achieve a best-selling or hot new release accolade (which can be extremely useful in ongoing book promotion).
- Be a door opener for you to connect with influencers and leaders who also reach your target reader.
- Create buzz and assist you in solidifying mentions and interviews through macro and micro media platforms.
- Support future book purchases online through a slew of meaningful reviews, letting both your future ideal readers and Amazon know that your book is worthy of being read, invested in and promoted.
- Position you with meaningful testimonials, insights and creative marketing opportunities for ongoing book promotion.
- Give you an opportunity to celebrate your awesome accomplishment. Don't ever miss the opportunity to relish in achieving this massive goal! You deserve it.

Whenever I think of a book launch, I hear Steven Tyler of Aerosmith singing in the background as the rocket prepares for launch.[4] People are nervous. Time is precious. Moments matter, as does preparation. There's a buildup. And the moment it launches, everyone is holding their breath. Until it's out there and there's no turning back.

Your book launch can be like that—and there are parts of it that should, for sure—but the good news is that it shouldn't cause you to have issues breathing, create constant worry or panic and feel like once it's gone, it's gone. Instead, book launches should give you flexibility for excitement, momentum for all the greatness ahead and energy to propel forward.

WANT A SUCCESSFUL BOOK LAUNCH?

Here are my top tips. There are actually many more, but let's start with my three favorites. They are ones that, when done well, can build a promotional pyramid higher than you've ever seen a cheerleading group accomplish.

Book Launch Tip #1: emPower others to join you.

There are many things you will have to do alone in life. Like having a tonsillectomy (I know this one from experience). Or asking for a pay raise (I prayed my dad could do this on my behalf in my early twenties, but to no avail). And even finding happiness (this is so true because until you decide you want it, you'll never see it even if it's sitting right in front of you).

While many things require you, alone, to make it happen, there are countless others that don't.

Like walking across the Red River Gorge's Natural Bridge. As a gal terrified of heights, I became immobilized when I hiked to the top of this beautiful landmark in Kentucky for the first time. I was trying to be brave, but my wobbly knees told a different story. I thought to cross the bridge and continue to hike required me to do it alone, but I was wrong. My husband and a dear friend interlocked their arms into mine and, together, we walked across a bridge that I was just sure the next wind would blow us off. (Hint: It didn't and because of their support, I got to see some of Kentucky's most beautiful land!)

Having a baby feels like a solitary act. You grow a baby in your body, and you're the one that has to evict him or her from their comfy space. But it requires a team to do so. Doulas have made a business of it. Spouses and partners help too. I know holding my husband's hand throughout the delivery of all three of our littles was critical. And the nurses and doctors, let's just say that by our third, I handpicked our nurse team (because I had so many kiddos they all knew me by name) and together we celebrated a miracle.

Birthing (and launching) a book is another team sport. If you think you can do it alone, guess again. Books aren't meant to be written in hiding, never to be shared with others. Neither are launches. EmPowering other people to join you on the launch journey isn't just a nicety, it's a requirement to a successful launch. And, let me tell you, they want to be on the journey with you! When you emPower them with how they can help you, that's where the magic happens.

Book Launch Tip #2: emPower others to help you.

There's nothing worse than wanting to help someone but not knowing how because they won't tell you what they need. It's like when I'm not feeling well, and I think that telepathically my husband should know what I want for dinner. Or when I don't get that perfect gift for my birthday because I never told anyone what I'd like. And what about when you write a book you want the world to know about, but you, yourself, don't tell a single soul.

I hate to break it to you, but you aren't telepathic. Your mouth moves to form words meant to be shared. There are people who know you, who love you and who want you to succeed that would love for you to tell them exactly what you want them to do so they can help you.[5]

When I was writing my book, I leveraged a launch team to help spread the word. I was nervous about what they would say, but I was more motivated by what they had the power to do. I knew many of my connections had been following my journey for years and were curious what I had up my sleeve. I knew they wanted to help me be successful in this new endeavor of mine. But what surprised me was how quickly they all assembled and took action when I emPowered them to help me.

Reflect on *why* you wrote your book.

As you remember what called you to choose a book as a tool for accomplishing your goal, consider how other people could help you achieve it. Don't audit your ideas; capture them all. Then pick your top three most important. Those should be what you emPower your launch team to help you with.

Book Launch Tip #3: emPower others to connect you.

When you think about marketing, I'd venture to say you get a sick feeling in the pit of your stomach. You likely think of "all the things" that you could be doing, should be doing, why in the world aren't you doing?! It feels overwhelming and confusing. You aren't alone. Ninety percent or so of authors we work with go through the same spiraling of emotions and worries.

When many think of marketing, they think of building relationships with cold leads, people who haven't a clue who you are. What if you flipped that idea upside down? What if, instead, you used your warm and hot leads (those who already know you and think you're cool) to reach out on your behalf to your cold leads? Let me explain.

Think about the last time you purchased a book. What pushed you to purchase it? I'll give you three guesses and the first two don't count. That's because I'm pretty confident it's because either you love the author and their work already (Mitch Albom and Jodi Picoult… one day I will meet you all, I know it!) or someone you trust recommended it.

The book selection I have been accumulating is due to these two reasons, and the first reason is really emPacted by the second. I didn't even know who Jodi Picoult was until a friend recommended *My Sister's Keeper*. Now, I'm on a quest to own every one of her books. And if it weren't for my high school, I might not know Mitch Albom exists. *Tuesdays With Morrie* was beautiful, but his other works have been even better. I can't imagine my life without his perspective.

The people who need your book are likely just a degree or two away from you right now. There are people who are in your network who believe in your message and would love a copy of your book. They would also love to share information about your book to others, recommending you and connecting with you along the way. Let them!

READY. SET. LAUNCH!

If launch day is different from release day, that means that you aren't really bound by time. Sure, momentum tends to pick up when the book is "new," but you hold the power to relaunch your book, even months or years after the release day. And when you emPower people to join you, help you and connect you, you are bound to launch to success.

Give me an "L." Give me an "A." Give me a "U." Oh, who am I kidding?! Cheerleading isn't in my blood, but launching is! Rah-rah! Go team! You've got this!

---

emPowered Thoughts

Have you set a launch date? Remember, you get to choose this day. It doesn't have to be similar to your book's release date. Choose a day that makes sense, gives you time to prepare and you get excited about.

What are some ways you *want* to launch your book? I get into specifics in *The emPowered Author Podcast* (so be sure to check it out), but a few to consider could be:

- Hosting an in-person or virtual launch event. Celebrate with your loved ones. Sell and sign books! Savor the feelings of success.
- Coordinate with a library, bookstore or business to host a launch event.
- Plan out a content strategy to ensure your social media connections know about your message.
- Create strategic partnerships and leverage your message to align with theirs. Beautiful things happen when people come together.

What are your launch success metrics? When I launched my first book, I held three in-person events where I sold all my book inventory. It felt amazing! But I realize everyone has their own success metrics with launch, and those should (and will) be directional in how you plan your launch efforts.

---

1. Need a shot of motivational realism? Reread chapter 5 and remember to look down, not up.
2. *Bring It On* is a cheerleading movie series I have to acknowledge I've actually watched.
3. Deep breaths. We will discuss launch teams in chapter 14.
4. *Armageddon* is a classic movie, and Aerosmith is probably one of my favorite bands of all time. So, you know, of course I'd jump to that.
5. If this excites you, chapter 14 will emPower you!

CHAPTER 14
EMPOWERING THOSE WHO WANT YOU TO SUCCEED

There is a single reason, I believe, book launches became the cornerstone of the emPower PR Group's original offerings, and it wasn't what I used to think it was.

At first, when authors began to reach out for marketing support specifically around their book launch, I used to think it was because I held an industry secret to book launch success:

- Maybe I've uncovered the diamond in the rough, I thought. Nah... I really don't think that's the reason.
- Possibly it's because marketing is complicated, I would tell myself. True, marketing is nuanced, but I still don't think that's why.
- What about the fact it's just hard to figure out the next right move with all this book writing, publishing and marketing stuff. That's it, I would consider! While that's accurate, I still think the reason is simpler than that.

After working with a multitude of authors, I think I've figured out the secret. *The reasons so many authors seek out book marketing launch support isn't merely for the technical and directional support, but for the emotional support too.* It's hard—emotionally—pulling together a group of people to help you launch your book to success (especially when you are so close to it yourself).

I WAS ONCE ASKED WHAT CHARACTER TRAITS WERE INSTRUMENTAL IN MY BOOK LAUNCH SUCCESS.

After reflecting on the question, I had the epiphany that I was just like each and every author I get to work with. In fact, these character traits not only help authors write marketable books, but it's what helps them bring the physical book to life and into the hands of those who need it most.

Vulnerability.

I find the best nonfiction books require the author to be vulnerable. With my first book being a memoir, I get it. Vulnerability was at the heart of each word I wrote. I shared stories that could have been embarrassing, but I knew that those stories were important to share, so I did. I was vulnerable about loss and heartache, but I knew there would be someone out there who needed to hear that message to get through their day, so I shared anyway.

Writing a book is a vulnerable experience in and of itself, but when the author is vulnerable, it creates connections. I remember being up in the middle of the night writing an extremely challenging chapter in my first book and, upon completion, I let out a massive, ugly cry. My husband woke up and came running, thinking I had fallen, gone into labor (yes, I was writing during pregnancy insomnia) or something much worse. It was quite the opposite. I shared that for once I felt free from something I had been carrying around alone. Sharing in such a vulnerable way was freeing for me. I looked at him and said, "I don't know why I have to share this story and this book, but I believe someone out there in the middle of the night may need this. If just one person benefits from my vulnerability, it was worth it."

A few months after the book was published, I received a message from a reader. It was in the middle of the night, so I didn't sit with the message until the morning, but when I did, I found myself in tears.

The woman shared she had been going through a hard time in her life and found herself, in the middle of the night, having anxiety attacks. This particular night, she felt one coming on, so she grabbed her Kindle and crawled into her closet. It just so happened my book was on her Kindle, and she shared that within fifteen minutes of reading it, she was able to breathe normally again. "You saved me," she shared. I didn't expect that my book—and my vulnerability—could emPower and inspire someone at that level. But I knew then the power a book can have on another.

Persistence.

Writing a book isn't for the fainthearted. It's exhausting—both physically and emotionally. Sharing your heart in the written format is so cathartic, but it takes time. It can suck you of your energy. It can rob you of moments with your loved ones, especially when you get inspired and can't put the pen down! There are times when you want to quit. There are moments when you get feedback, and you want to walk away from it all. There are those who judge you for doing something you love and others who downright don't believe in you. That's when persistence needs to kick in.

I was so excited about my message that I originally shared parts of it through my blog. In fact, it was my blog readers who began to demand I write a book. So, when I packaged up my manuscript and shared it with my editorial board of beta readers, I expected only glorious feedback. I was confident. I was excited. And I knew the manuscript was strong.

However, the feedback I received—while I'm grateful for it now—offered some areas for rework and growth opportunities. Because I wasn't expecting to receive this feedback—or maybe it was because I hadn't grown thick skin quite yet—I found myself speechless. Instead of listening to their feedback and taking action to level up my manuscript, I put it away for months.

A near-finished manuscript sat and collected dust because I was too proud to accept feedback. Several months later, only after a major shift happened in my professional life, I picked up the manuscript and the feedback with a new set of eyes. I realized the feedback shared was amazing and was meant to make my strong manuscript *great*. I came back to it with a newfound energy and didn't just publish a book, I launched an Amazon best seller!

Writing a book can be a vulnerable experience and definitely requires persistence. But the truth is writing the book is just fine-tuning your traits so you are prepared to launch.

LAUNCHING A BOOK REQUIRES A HEALTHY DOSE OF VULNERABILITY AND PERSISTENCE TOO.

I know too many authors who write a book that is brilliant and honest, game-changing and meaningful, full of value and full of wisdom. Yet, they don't tell anyone about it. They write in silence, and they launch in silence, hoping someone may stumble upon their book and it will go viral without them telling a single person.

I hate to break it to you, but that's flawed thinking.

Our world is noisy and crowded. It's full of message sharing constantly. Lives are filled to the brim. People are overwhelmed. The potential of someone stumbling upon your brilliance is not just a one-in-a-million chance, it's probably a one-in-a-billion. The odds aren't in your favor.

If you want to sell books, you're going to have to talk about them. You're going to have to tell people you wrote it. You're going to have to share that you did something so few do and so many want to. It's going to require you to be vulnerable (gulp) and persistent (ugh). It means you are going to have to tell those who know you that you accomplished this amazing undertaking first!

You know the analogy many refer to when you find yourself overwhelmed and you aren't sure how to tackle it? *You know how to eat an elephant? One bite at a time.* Tackle the biggest project first and then use the fun tasks as your reward. When it comes to launching your book, I'd like to adapt that concept a bit. To launch a book, you have to go backward to go forward. It's counterintuitive. It's against everything you want to do. And it requires you to be vulnerable with people who know you (which is scarier to do than to be vulnerable with people who don't). But it's how you will move forward with energy and momentum.

PEOPLE WANT TO HELP YOU, BUT THEY JUST DON'T KNOW HOW. TELL THEM.

You can invest in advertising or secure interviews on your local TV station. You can host a podcast or guest on others'. You can go on the road and tell your story to anyone and everyone who will listen. But if you don't tell those who already know you, love you, believe in you and want you to succeed about your book, you're missing a major group of people who are already on board to help but haven't a clue how to do it.

I call these people your warm leads, and they make amazing launch team members.

Ever heard of a book launch team? Some call it a street team or an army of supporters. I've always said I don't care what you call me, just make sure you call me for dinner, and call me to be a part of your book launch!

One of my tried-and-true methods to help sell books and create a large emPact is through a launch team. Whatever you want to call it is merely semantics. The end result is the same—when you rally together a group of individuals who know you, love you and want you and your book to succeed, magic happens.

To help you consider how to emPower those who want you to succeed to do so, let's consider the W's of a book launch team: the Who, What, When, Where and How.

The Whos of a Launch Team

A book launch team should be comprised of a group of people who don't need any convincing you are awesome and your book is meaningful. They already know it because they know you and they want to help you achieve your goals. They are warm leads. They will likely already buy your book if they haven't already and would be honored to help you do more with it.

Your launch team could be comprised of your family and your friends. It could include your neighbors or members of your church, social organization or network. You could invite your current or previous coworkers to it. These people could know you extremely well or only know a part of you. They may remember the days when you were in diapers or have just met you last week. There is no parameter of who the who's should be except that they should be supporters of you.

That's it. Easy, right?!

Wrong! Asking those who *know* you to support you in this way is a vulnerable experience. Many will exceed any expectation you have, and many will unintentionally let you down. (They remember you decades ago when you were in diapers, remember?! They don't realize that you are the amazing thought leader that you are today.)

It's not easy. It will require you to be vulnerable. But it's worth it.

The What of a Launch Team

A launch team can be used for various purposes in a book promotional strategy. However, the primary purpose being to ensure the book makes a splash on various platforms during the launch and provide ongoing publicity post-launch.

To clarify your launch team's success, ask yourself these questions:

- What could a launch team do for me?
- What do I hope they will accomplish?
- How will I know if the launch team is successful?

Here are a few ideas on how a launch team could help you.[1]

- A launch team could assist you in reaching an Amazon review goal early in the book launch phase (which could help in getting Amazon to organically start promoting the book).

- They could assist you in achieving an Amazon best seller accolade (which you could use in promotion later).
- A group of supporters could provide you extended visibility to their connections through social media promotion.
- One of my favorite ways they could help is by connecting you with individuals who may be interested in purchasing your book, inviting you to come as a speaker or introducing you to a strategic partner.

The what of a launch team varies from author to author, and only you can determine what you would find their help most successful with. However, a pro tip is to ensure the launch team knows exactly what you want their help with from the beginning.

The When of a Launch Team

I love using launch teams to launch or relaunch a book, so the *when* of a launch team can vary. That said, the best time to bring a launch team on board is a few months prior to your book launch. This gives you time to slowly bring them up to speed on what you've been spending hours, days, weeks, months and maybe even years creating.

I feel like eight to twelve weeks is enough time to build pre-launch, launch and post-launch efforts with your team and not have them lose steam along the way. Remember, the people on your launch team have lives and jobs and priorities. They love you and want you to succeed, but they have other things happening too. When you think about the timing of your launch team, keep in mind that a focused and concentrated effort that allows for methodical movement is important and realistic.

The Where of a Launch Team

You have the whos figured out, and you've got plenty of them! (I recommend shooting for between fifty and two hundred people.) You know what you want them to help you with and you know when you want their help. Where is a big unknown for most authors—where will you all connect?

We live in a digital world where digital connection happens on the daily. Your launch team can work that way too, and it should. I always recommend you consider two wheres to engage with your launch team—one that allows you to communicate in a one-to-one way (usually via email) and one that creates a community (usually via an online group). You will want to share information but also allow your group to get innovative together.

The How of a Launch Team

How in the world do you make a launch team successful? Here are my top ten how tips.

1. *Be authentic.* Be you. Your launch team doesn't need to be persuaded to know you are awesome. They know it already!
2. *Be relevant.* Whenever you can make your book and your message relevant to your launch team, they will be more engaged and more likely to tell others.
3. *Be focused.* Whether you like clear direction or not, your launch team needs and deserves it. Identify three ways they can help you most and stick to them.
4. *Be respectful.* Your launch team members are helping you, not working for you. Be respectful, gracious and humble.
5. *Be limited.* Keep to your timeline and let people know when you have accomplished what you set out to do together.
6. *Be extra.* Make your launch team feel special. Think of ways to give them insider peeks of your journey; they will love it!
7. *Be open.* Vulnerability is key. Let them in on how you are feeling, what this journey is like for you and how their help means the world.
8. *Be focused on them.* Make their life easy and if you do, they will make your launch a piece of cake. What can you do to help them help you more?
9. *Be engaged.* The best launch teams are ones where the launch team members and the author are engaged regularly with one another.

10. *Be a good listener.* Your launch team will give you beta feedback and open opportunities you didn't know existed. Be nimble enough to take action when new and unexpected doors open.

I end every episode of *The emPowered Author Podcast* with a single sentence, but it's the most important one that I ever say:

EmPowered people emPower people.

If you want to become an emPowered author, you should start by emPowering people. EmPowerment requires vulnerability and persistence, but it pays off. When you emPower your connections, they are prepped and ready to become a street army of supporters who will help your message ripple extend farther than you could ever do yourself.

---

emPowered Thoughts

How have you told your connections about your book? Have you mentioned it? Are they aware? If they are, consider if there are meaningful ways to continue to spread the word. If you have kept this goodness for yourself, reflect on why.

How could you use a launch team to help you achieve your book marketing goals? Revisit part one in this book and remember your *why*. Your launch team can help you accomplish it.

It's time to build out your book launch team plan. Our team at the emPower PR Group would love to help you if you'd like, or you can take the insights shared in this chapter to roll up your sleeves and get to work!

---

1. I encourage you to go to your book success goals and metrics and leverage them here too.

CHAPTER 15
GET SEEN. BE HEARD. SELL BOOKS.

There were three Post-it notes, each with two simple words written clearly in permanent marker. They didn't need any additional context, for the action required was straightforward enough. Even if I wanted to beg for more context or direction, there was no getting it, because this insight came in a dream. Literally.

I've become accustomed to getting some of my favorite life-changing insights from literal dreams.[1] This one came in a more recent one. Those three Post-its, I realized quickly, were the distilled essence of a visibility strategy:

- Get seen.
- Be heard.
- Sell books.

I woke up, sipped my chai tea latte and simmered on the message a bit longer. As with most dreams (and most movies based on books), there's always more to the story. And there's always more to any visibility strategy, especially one that works!

Most authors love to hop right to visibility marketing efforts upon their book's release. They want to get their books into libraries and bookstores. They want to speak on stages and in book clubs. Podcasts and television stations should be calling any day, right? Netflix fans, get ready, because their book is going to be the newest top-rated movie. All of these efforts are exciting and some very important for sure but, whether you want to hear this simple truth or not, I'm going to say it. Putting energy into visibility strategy development and execution should be third on your priority list.[2]

VISIBILITY IS ABOUT RAISING AWARENESS OF YOU, YOUR BOOK AND YOUR MESSAGE.

At its purest form, it's all about getting seen. There are many ways you can accomplish that goal, as evidenced in how other businesses generate visibility with creative approaches.

- Ever seen an employee of a pizza company stand at the corner of a major intersection flipping a foam-core board with the specials of the day? They are definitely getting seen, especially when the employee takes great pride in the flipping tricks he has perfected.
- I'm sure you've driven by the larger-than-life flopping eyesores car lots love to use to generate visibility as you zoom by their establishment. My kids always loved watching the arms of those things flop in the wind.
- Billboards help you know if a Chick-fil-A or Cracker Barrel will be your dinner choice as you go on a road trip, and neighborhood coupon booklets always pique my family's interest when we are opting for a new dinner option.

In each of these scenarios, people (and businesses) are getting seen. But is it effective? Possibly, but I find myself watching the employee's mad flipping skills more than being drawn to get pizza that night, and when I'm ready to buy a car, it's not because I was inspired to do so while driving by. It may inspire me to consider what they have to offer, but it usually isn't what pushes me to action. I'm likely to do some research first (even if that research is quickly online to see if they have my favorite pizza choice on sale).

If you want to sell books (and lots of them!) it is important to ensure you have a solid author platform first. Visibility with no clear direction is a missed opportunity and never creates the outcome you hope for. If you have a strong author platform—one that directs people easily to book sales and whatever else you offer—your goal of book sales can and will be accomplished.

There's another important but often overlooked aspect to a visibility strategy for authors. You can try flipping a board and putting a yard decoration out to spur book sales, but I'm pretty certain it won't generate the interest you seek. Getting seen is only half of the battle. The word visible is the root word of visibility, but effective visibility isn't just about getting seen; it's also about being heard. The best visibility strategies require your message to be absorbed to be effective and emPowering. Someone merely *seeing* you may not be spurred to action. But if you are *heard*, too, that's where book sales happen.

How do you accomplish both? Let's dissect each.

GETTING SEEN

For some authors, this part of a visibility strategy goes against everything they *want* to do. Writing a book is something you can do in the quiet of your home, away from lights, cameras and action. A book is a beacon of knowledge, but it doesn't necessarily require the author of it to be the outward voice.

Or some authors think as much.

If you want to sell more books, you can't hide behind them. You need to become the megaphone for them! People connect with people. Books are a tool to communicate a message to another person. In truth, even the best of book lovers (and I may be one of them) realize that they aren't merely purchasing some pages bound together. They are investing in a message that a person took time to share.

Of course you want your book seen. But the best way to make that happen is through you. The best way to get your book seen is to ensure *you* are being seen. Here are some ideas to consider as you step out from behind your book and into the limelight.

Start by evaluating your connections.

- Who do you know who has a platform where it would make sense for you and your book to be highlighted?
- Who do you know who might be connected to someone who has a platform that makes sense for your message—and that of your book's—to be shared?
- How could your connections connect you with those who need your message?

Visibility strategies are about leveraging other people's platforms to grow yours. Many of your connections or your connections' connections are influencers who can help you get seen. However, it's important to never forget that the best visibility efforts are win-win solutions for all involved.

Leveraging someone else's platform to help you get seen requires you to realize you have a message and your story matters to an audience on another platform. Just like you, however, that influencer utilizes their platform for their own goals. Many times, goals collide. When they do, that's where the fireworks happen. If you can identify a way to become a value-add to another platform, you may become a solution to a problem of theirs.

Some believe in the six degrees of separation theory—that we can all be linked together in some way by a handful of connections. While that may be true, when it comes to a visibility strategy, I believe that the chain of connections between us and those who need our message isn't six degrees away. They may only be one or two, instead. In fact, usually your connections know individuals who have platforms that are open and willing to help spread the word about our message. The question isn't if they are there; it's if we will ask!

Your connections have connections. Who do they know and how can they help you?[3]

Another visibility opportunity comes by evaluating the groups you are a part of or the organization that you have joined. Where are your target readers engaged most? How could you be seen through their networks?

Being seen can look and feel different for every author, for every platform, for every message. Sometimes, being seen requires physical visibility: speaking engagements, television interviews, YouTube videos or networking events. Other times, being seen doesn't require people seeing your face. Instead, a podcast interview or a blog contribution can be just as helpful. Getting seen merely means generating awareness for your book and your message.

BEING HEARD

If someone sees you but doesn't hear your message, does it matter? It's like the riddle that asks if a tree falls in the forest with no one around does it make a sound? I believe that being seen but not heard misses the point. Being seen is the bait; being heard is the hook. I'll go for the hook any day.

Have you ever had a conversation with someone face-to-face where they are looking at you and watching your lips move, but they definitely weren't hearing what you had to say? Become a parent and you'll see this phenomenon on the daily. The glazed look in their eyes is an indication that you can keep talking, but they aren't listening.

They may be preoccupied with something else going on in their lives. Or they may be one of those people who are thinking of what they are going to say next instead of listening to what you are sharing with them first. Maybe they are tired or uninterested. Whatever the reason, it doesn't matter; you can get seen all you want, but you are definitely not being heard.

This is the key differentiator between just any visibility strategy and an effective one. Getting seen but not being heard is a recipe for a visibility strategy disaster. It won't work. Ever. It's wasted energy, and I'm sure you don't have any energy to waste. I know I don't. I could spend time writing more books, playing with my kids or taking a nap. There are a lot better efforts you could spend your time and energy on than a visibility strategy that falls flat.

To make sure your visibility efforts are worth it, you need to spur on conversations. They happen best when eyes and ears are both open.

How do you find people who aren't just seeing you, but open to listening as well?

Start by having clarity on your target reader and where they go for trusted information. The word *trusted* is pivotal. We all have a plan to gather trusted information, and if you can ensure you are getting seen through that source, you are more likely to have people who are willing to listen to what you have to say.

These trusted sources of information could be physical places—such as a church, an organization or a school. They could be virtual spaces—such as social media groups, influencers or networking sites. They could be people—such as uber connectors, thought leaders or media personalities.

If you know who your target reader is and where they go for trusted information, you will likely increase your visibility by being seen, and furthermore, getting heard! And in doing so, something magical will likely happen. You, author friend, will sell books!

SELLING BOOKS

Before you flipped through the pages of this book, I bet you thought selling books was easier than it really is. As with most things that matter in life, the most important efforts aren't always the easiest ones. You can sell a handful of books to your friends and family, but I want you to sell books far and wide because I know you have a message the world needs and will become transformed by.

For most nonfiction authors, selling books isn't really your endgame. It's an avenue to accomplish it. You are wanting to make an emPact—your author emPact—and book sales are a metric of measurement. It's a revenue stream and a tangible outcome of a goal that is hard to quantify. But it isn't the goal itself. Your goal is likely much, much bigger.

There are only so many hours in the day and unfortunately you and I can't have in-depth conversations with every single person we know will benefit from what we feel called to share. A book allows us to rest our vocal cords while still making a large emPact.

A bookstore sells books—and they may be able to sell yours! But without a visibility strategy aligned with promoting your book's availability in that bookstore, guess what?! You won't likely sell many. Your book is just one of thousands that you hope someone will walk in and pick up. (And guess what? Those other authors have the same wish for their books!)

You are selected to provide a keynote address at a conference! But what if you are on the wrong stage, and those in attendance did not come with their ears open to hear what you have to share? I would venture to say you can chock up that experience to stage practice instead of seeing book sales come from it.

A TV station invites you to be interviewed on their morning show! Such fun, but your segment is just a few minutes and what if your target readers aren't their primary audience? Or what if you don't leverage the opportunity to share with your connections? Again, I'll be the one to say what you and I know will happen. You probably aren't going to see a spike in book sales.

A visibility strategy that allows you to be seen and heard will help you sell books. It's truly that simple.

BOOKS DON'T SELL THEMSELVES.

People do. You do. And the best way to do that is to get seen and be heard. Because the hook leads to book sales. Book sales lead to value giving. Value giving leads to piqued interest. Piqued interest leads to book sales. Book sales lead to business growth. And it all leads to extended reach and greater author emPact.

---

emPowered Thoughts

How can you get seen? This is the part of the visibility strategy authors get excited about. It's shiny and fun (for the most part). But I want to challenge you to evaluate opportunities to increase your visibility where those who need and want your book most will be watching (and listening).

How can you be heard? Open eyes and closed ears will get you nowhere. What platforms can you leverage to spread your message where your target readers will be most receptive?

How can you sell books? If you want to reach many, there is nothing easy about it. But it can be done and you can make it happen.

---

1. Remember, my first book was inspired by a life-changing dream.
2. Only after you have a strong author platform and leverage your connections should you dive into visibility efforts.
3. Never forget that they would likely love to support you in this way.

PART FOUR
BUILD OR GROW A BUSINESS

authorpreneur (n): an author who realizes and embraces that the moment they wrote a book they were forming a business and they are equipped to do so

CHAPTER 16
A BOOK CAN BE THE BEGINNING OF A BUSINESS

"What would you be doing if you weren't doing this?"

It was the beginning of a conversation that would forever change the trajectory of my career and, coincidentally, my life.

Marie had become one of my closest coworkers, even though we worked on two sides of the United States and spent months building a working relationship without meeting in person. These were the days before video conferencing was readily accessible, so all we had to go on was conversation and trust. We quickly built both.

I had a feeling changes were coming. They always are. Change is just next door, waiting for a crack to expose your comfort zone and push you outside of it. It doesn't like you to feel warm and fuzzy. It gets excited when your adrenaline pumps. Change and me weren't always friends, but now she's a welcomed member at my Thanksgiving table.

She wasn't back then, and when I got wind that the organization I had expected to retire from had more corporate layoffs on the horizon, I called Marie to acknowledge the uncomfortable feeling I had in the pit of my stomach. I knew it was coming. I knew we couldn't dodge it forever. I feared we might be impacted by the next round of layoffs.

No one is ever safe and, many times, we are all chess pieces in the game Life is playing. After wallowing in self-pity for a brief bout of what-ifs, Marie and I switched the story and, instead, talked about what we would do if we weren't doing what we were currently doing (follow that tongue twister?!). The question proved hard to answer.

"I have no idea," was the best response I could offer. Because the answer felt daunting, I decided to propose a different question.

"What do you think I should do if it's not this?" Her answer shocked me.

"YOU SHOULD BLOG."

Because, you know, there's money in that industry... Not!

Marie was so confident in her answer, but I wasn't. I laughed at her response, asking how that would put food on the table. She didn't have the answers, but there was a persistence in her voice. She kept telling me I needed to write. There was something she knew I needed to tell the world.

She had no clue I already was writing. I had started writing when I felt like I couldn't clear my head of its clutter. I had started writing when interesting experiences happened that I just didn't want to forget. Writing became my outlet, but I hadn't told many about it.

The next day—after considering her suggestion—I dialed Marie's number. "Challenge accepted," I said. I wasn't going to wait to be impacted by a layoff to start a blog. I decided to start one that day. I began to blog about the experiences I had been writing about and, surprisingly, as I began sharing my blog, a new demand came of me; the request to purchase a book (a book, mind you, I never planned to write).

I'll spare you the nitty-gritty details on how it all transpired, but it's a story that I wouldn't believe if I hadn't experienced it firsthand. Coincidentally, years after I began blogging, I *was* impacted by a layoff.

While an entire manuscript was prepped and ready to publish, I didn't move forward with it until I was thrust into the uncomfortable, jobless land of unemployment. I figured, what's the worst that could happen? However, I should have been asking myself, what's the best?!

THE OUTCOME OF WRITING A BOOK ISN'T JUST THE BOOK ITSELF; IT'S ALSO A BUSINESS.

A week or so before my book launched, I was charged with sharing my launch plan with my book coaching cohort. I was nervous, but I made it happen. I pulled together the ideas I had to take something meaningful to me and make it meaningful to others. In the middle of my favorite lunch spot, I borrowed their free Wi-Fi, ate a delicious grilled cheese and did a virtual presentation of my launch plan.

That day, I'll always remember. I'll always remember how I realized my favorite lunch place needed to stay just that, my favorite lunch place. It didn't need a new title, like "the place you host a virtual webinar." It was loud, and I was so distracted. It wasn't a peaceful Starbucks by any stretch of the imagination.

I was so proud of my newly branded PowerPoint slides.[1] I'll always remember my heart racing because, even though I am comfortable in front of crowds, I am not comfortable being vulnerable. And writing a book (and marketing it) when the message hits close to home isn't easy.

But what I remember most were the calls I got afterward from my book coach and publisher. I thought I was in trouble. That's my guilty conscience for you. But, instead, it was an opportunity. They both saw something in me I hadn't seen in myself. I knew my book was meant for more than reading. I was open to the idea of speaking on the topics found within it. But I never expected my book to be the launch of a business.

YOUR BUSINESS COULD BE JUST ONE BOOK AWAY.

My book launch was successful. My book (and the many others since) continues to inspire people. I've spoken to small groups and large ones, bringing the page to the stage. I envisioned that would happen. I was open to those opportunities. But I never expected to merge my love for books and my skill set in marketing to build the emPower PR Group. I don't think anyone could. But my book made that happen, and your book has the power to do the same for you.

Whether you want to admit it or not, writing a book is the beginning of launching a business. There are things you learn that only entrepreneurs and business owners have to tackle.

You learn all about sales tax and EINs. You figure out the importance of having a PO Box and ask yourself questions about whether you need an LLC or not. (Too many three-letter acronyms to deal with!) You start carrying inventory (and keep some in your trunk because you never want to be without a few books to sell in a Walmart parking lot. It feels sketchy, but not for long!). You learn how to process credit card transactions from your phone because the phrase—"I'd love to buy a book, but I don't have cash"—should never hinder a book sale.

Beyond the logistical requirements, you begin to think about things like metrics and goals and create strategies to achieve them. You reflect on worthy investments to further your book sales, and you begin to hear from your readers about what other opportunities exist.

- Could you provide one-on-one coaching packages or book club reflection guides?
- What about retreats either hosted by you or ones that you speak at?
- Speaking of speaking, people start asking you what your speaker fees are (and you didn't even know that was a thing until they asked!).

You, my friend, are unexpectedly launching not just a book, but also a business. I call those of us who are uniquely poised with a book and a business, authorpreneurs! Welcome to the cool club.

THERE ARE SEVERAL REASONS YOU MAY FIND THIS TERRIFYING AND EXHILARATING.

Maybe, like me, you didn't have the entrepreneurial spirit. At first, anyway. If you have a message to share and you feel called to write it, you are already being vulnerable. Why not add a side of business management to the mix?

Maybe you love your nine-to-five and couldn't imagine leaving it. Well, guess what? Many people manage two career paths at once nowadays. Look at all the mid-level marketing companies out there. I'm sure there's a stat that proves most people are doing it.

Maybe you'd love to kick your nine-to-five job to the curb. A book could be the start of something bigger. I've seen the power of a book and how it changes others; how it's changed me. If you are wanting to start something new, a book could be the gateway to it.

What if you are already an entrepreneur? A book could help grow your business. You could evolve from "the person who runs XYZ company" to "the person who wrote the book that the XYZ company is based upon." Now that has a ring to it!

A book has the power to elevate (figuratively, not literally). It distinguishes you from your competition and it gives you an opportunity to let people taste test your offerings. From a tapas lover over here, trust me when I say, many people who taste your book appetizer will decide you are the real deal and worth investing in.

EVERY AUTHOR IS REALLY AN AUTHORPRENEUR.

Behind the book is an author.
Behind an author is an authorpreneur.

I love helping authorpreneurs (like you) identify how to build (or grow) their businesses to work for them in alignment with their books.[2] As you consider how a book can be the beginning of a business, here are a few insights to keep close.

- Never forget the value of your book and use it strategically to help you grow your business. Your readers will tell you the value, and, if you are listening closely, you can find your business nugget within their feedback.
- Build a business that is sustainable, inspiring to you and built with systems and structures that allow for effective and ongoing marketing efforts.
- Gain clarity on your business offerings and ensure your promotional efforts are in alignment. This doesn't happen overnight but, instead, over time. Become comfortable with slow, methodical movement and constant refinement.
- Grow your reach to your target audience—those who need you, want you and will invest in you. To have an effective business requires your target audience to do all three.

This may be uncharted territory, but rest assured some uncharted territory is merely waiting for *you* to chart it. It's a new beginning. The sky is literally the limit. The opportunities are endless. Your future awaits. (And so does your business, authorpreneur!)

---

emPowered Thoughts

What are your readers telling you? Usually, they know the business you should build before you do. Are you listening to them? Do you have a way for them to share with you their thoughts and, better yet, their needs?

Have you ever considered forming a business from your book's message? Does this concept exhilarate you or terrify you? Either emotion is normal (as are all emotions in between). Listen to how you are feeling and consider why you feel that way. What could be holding you back? (Hint: It could be yourself.)

What authorpreneur unknowns do you need to uncover? You don't have to know all the things; just know who can help you learn what you don't know. Make a list of your questions and start identifying who can help you answer each.

---

1. Y'all! They matched my book cover, and I thought they were fantabulous.
2. This is also a specialty of the emPower PR Group.

CHAPTER 17
THE AUTHORPRENEUR EQUATION

Authorpreneur may be a tongue twister, but becoming one isn't an overcomplicated process. In fact, it only takes three steps:

1. You have a message to share and something people will value.
2. You write a book as a conduit to share your message.
3. You build or grow a business from your message and alongside your book.

It's that easy! Well, not entirely… but the execution of authorpreneurship doesn't have to break the bank, overwhelm your already chaotic life or leave you immobilized and unsure of your next right step.

ALL YOU HAVE TO DO IS SOLVE THE AUTHORPRENEUR EQUATION.

When I was a senior in high school, I had no clue what I wanted to do for a living. My childhood dreams no longer enticed me. So I began grasping for straws.

"I think I want to major in math and be a math teacher," I had told my dad one day.

If he had been drinking coffee, I'm sure he would have spit it out when I said this. "Stephanie? A math major? What has come of this world?"

Now, to my credit, I was acing my college calculus course, and algebra I and II had been some of my favorite classes. I loved equations and solving for the unknown. The only problem was my basic math skills were lacking. Basic adding and subtracting requires a calculator because I was taught how to use them versus how to formulate mathematical answers internally in grade school. Outside of that, give me a challenging equation and I love the black and white nature of solving it.

I didn't become a math major, obviously! But I did bring math into the work I get to do now. This equation, however, doesn't require a degree to solve, but in uncovering the unknown, books sell, messages are shared and businesses are formed.

YOUR VALUE + THEIR NEEDS = MARKETABLE SOLUTION

I don't need a calculator to solve this equation. Instead, I need a message of value, audience insights and a willingness to listen to a need and take action accordingly. Let's dig in.

Your Value

Ever wondered what you have that someone else may not? On the surface, you may not think that you or what you have to bring is unique. Anyone can write a book. Anyone can highlight a skill that you have. Why would anyone invest in you over another person?

Great questions. I asked the same questions when I formed my wreath business. Why would someone buy a wreath from *me* when they could visit Target and get one cheaper and more quickly? There are tons of wreath makers out there; what made me special?

The answer was simple. *Me.*

I was the differentiator. I was the one who brought my perspective to each wreath I made. I was the one who would work tirelessly with my customers to create a unique wreath just for them that no one else had.

I was the creator of memorial wreaths and birthday wreaths. I was what was different.

You are what makes your message, your book and your business different.

It can be hard to see the best in yourself, so ask your friends, family, readers, peers and clients what they value most in you. As you listen, uncover what part of your value people will invest in.

Their Needs

Brownies. Need I say more?[1] When it comes to determining what your potential clients will invest in, you need to uncover their *needs*. There is a difference between a want and a need. From a marketing perspective, you want to ensure your authorpreneur business efforts meet the *needs* of those who find value in what you bring to the conversation.

Resources are limited, and when it comes to deciding how to invest one's resources—whether conscious or not—we all begin with our needs first. Ensuring that your business aligns with those needs means you are giving your business the best chance for growth and opportunity.

Unsure what the needs of your target clients are? Ask them! Watch their spending behavior. Listen and do so frequently. They will tell you.

Marketable Solution

When you merge your value with the needs of those who will invest in you, you identify your marketable solution. Your book is likely one of many solutions. And your business is likely another.

What value do you bring that others will buy from you? That's a marketable solution. What is a need of your target audience that you offer and they will invest in? Another marketable solution. What message do you have? What's a unique skill you can share that meets a need? Guess what? You've figured out a marketable solution.

ANYONE CAN WRITE A BOOK. ANYONE CAN FORM A BUSINESS. BUT NOT EVERYONE WILL DO IT SUCCESSFULLY.

Due to the wonderful world of self-publishing, it's easy for anyone to write and publish a book (even if the book is missing the marketable mark). I've met many people who form a business who probably shouldn't have. Not everyone *will* do both successfully, but everyone *could*. This is living, breathing proof that you *can* do anything, including build or grow a business with a book utilizing the authorpreneur equation.

I get the opportunity to work with authors who want to write or leverage a book to build or grow a business and do so effectively. Every time I get the chance to do so, I go back to the Author emPact Framework.[2] When leveraging the Framework, here's what I focus on:

- There are three reasons most people want to write a book.
- Understanding your *why* will help you figure out where to put your energy.
- From there, uncover solutions to help you accomplish your *why*.

If you want to embrace all that authorpreneurship offers, you'll need to write a marketable book, sell more books and be open to building or growing a business. All parts of the Framework will need to work together in unison.

The beginning of authorpreneurship doesn't require you to have the same starting point as another person. It can begin where you are. And I'm guessing you probably identify with one of these three statements:

- You haven't written a book yet, but you want to.
- You have written a book, but you haven't created a business from it yet.
- You have a business already, but you haven't written a book and you realize a book could help you grow your business.

No matter where you are on this journey, I have some tips to help you move closer to fully embracing everything that being an authorpreneur offers.

YOU HAVEN'T WRITTEN A BOOK YET, BUT YOU WANT TO.

Yay! That makes my heart happy for many reasons, but the biggest is that you get the opportunity to not just write any book… but to write a marketable one.

If you are looking to write a book to build a business, here are some tips.

- Leverage your expertise to inspire, engage and evoke action. You bring value; allow your book to share it.
- Write a book the people you want to work with and for *need*. This will draw people to you and your business.
- Write to your reader. Realize the first draft of your book is likely for you; the second draft is for them.
- Write a book you can use in your business. Consider how you will use your book within your business.
- Write a book that can open doors. How can your book be used to connect you with those who could use your services?

YOU HAVE WRITTEN A BOOK, BUT YOU HAVEN'T CREATED A BUSINESS FROM IT YET.

You're in luck! It's time to create a marketable business. If you've written a book, now how can you use it to build a business from it?

If you are looking to use a book to build a business, here are some tips.

- Hone in on your unique expertise. What makes you different from another who is speaking on your topic, writing books to your target readers or serving clients directly with their services?

- Listen to what your readers are still wanting. Your readers and potential clients want to get seen and be heard too. Listen! They will tell you what they need.
- Identify what type of business *you* want to create. The most successful businesses, in my opinion, are those that offer value and ones the owners love sharing.
- What derivative offerings can you provide? Do you want to be a coach or consultant, offer an online course, become a speaker, etc.? Consider how you can lift the message from your book and share it in different ways.

YOU HAVE A BUSINESS ALREADY, BUT YOU HAVEN'T WRITTEN A BOOK, AND YOU REALIZE A BOOK COULD HELP YOU GROW YOUR BUSINESS.

Books offer new ways to reach new and potential clients. If you already have a business, you may be missing out on an opportunity to reach people who need your message. Plus, you could up level as a thought leader by publishing a book.

If you are looking to grow your existing business with a book, here are some questions to reflect upon.

- What could you do more efficiently, and how can a book help you do that? A book could help your business run more smoothly.
- How could you use a book to get new business? How could a book become a door opener for you?
- How could you use a book to reach new people? Who could benefit from your message that isn't already?

You can write a book.
You can publish a book.
You can create a business.
But only authorpreneurs use their unique skills to do all three successfully.

---

emPowered Thoughts

What is your unique value? The first part of the authorpreneur equation is all about you and the unique value you bring to others. Do you know what that is? If not, who can you ask to help you uncover it?

What are their needs? Your target readers and clients have needs and when you know what they are, you are more likely to find the sweet spot so they will invest in your book.

What is your marketable solution? How can you make your value a solution to their needs? And it's not just any solution; I'm talking about a marketable one… one people are demanding and one they will buy.

---

1. If so, preheat the oven, whip up a batch of brownies and reread chapter 6.
2. Check out chapter 3 for a refresher of the Framework.

CHAPTER 18
TIME OVER MONEY OR MONEY OVER TIME

I trudged into my local craft store for the umpteenth time, pulling my rolling cart behind me. However, instead of purchasing products, I was headed to teach my craft to others. It was a day to create, and in my book, any day to create is a day that's bound to be exciting.

With loads of red, loosely woven burlap spools, a heart wreath frame, chevron ribbon and floral wire, I was set to teach a few dozen people some new skills. The burlap heart wreath they would make that day would be a memento of their ability to tackle something new and end up with a final product well worth the hard work.

I had frequented this craft store multiple times a week for several years, so I was well known as the wreath lady. I was fine with that; I was in heaven when wrapped up in burlap fabrics and gazing at whatever floral selections they had for the season. Many friendships were built from my creative business, but one in particular stuck.

A CASHIER HAD TAKEN AN INTEREST IN MY BLOOMING BUSINESS AND WOULD REGULARLY ASK BUSINESS TIPS AT CHECK OUT.

She, too, was a creator, but her medium was wood slivers; her craft, wood burnings. Her artistic eye created pure masterpieces. I was in awe of what she could do, and it was a pleasure to give her insights into how she could potentially grow her business.

That particular day, she was on break and offered to help me set up for the upcoming workshop. As we unpacked rolls of burlap and placed each person's materials meticulously by their spot at the table, she made an interesting comment.

"Stephanie," she asked, "aren't you afraid that if you teach people how to do something you are trying to sell that they won't want to purchase from you? Aren't you worried they will just make it themselves?"

In the beginning of hosting workshops, that fear of scarcity lingered in my thoughts, but I realized that my worries—and that of my creative pupil—had no merit. Instead, something quite the opposite happened.

The skillset I was teaching was one that *could* mean that I would lose business. Those in attendance *could* decide to make all the wreaths that their home would ever need. That definitely was a possibility. But it wasn't reality, and I used the moment as an opportunity to share with her my insights.

"There are two types of people," I explained, "those who value time over money and those who value money over time." She looked at me, perplexed, and I continued to explain what I had learned about my workshops, about my business and about my target audience.

SOME OF YOUR TARGET AUDIENCE WILL VALUE TIME OVER MONEY.

Early in my wreath business, I believed that those who would pay for my services wanted a finished piece. They wanted a beautiful, custom-made creation to hang on their door front as a welcoming piece of art. They wanted something they had a hand in selecting colors and design for, but they wanted my creative eye and my design aesthetic. They wanted *me* to create.

This subset of my target audience—those who were willing to invest in a custom wreath they couldn't pick up at their local craft store—were willing to invest in me and my work. They didn't want to peruse pre-made options, hoping to select something that *may* fit their needs at a potentially lower price point. They wanted to save time store hopping and were willing to invest in a custom piece made by yours truly. This group of people valued time (as they didn't want to spend it traveling around to find a perfect wreath for their space) over money (since they were willing to invest in a custom handmade piece to fit their needs).

The same mentality holds true in my book marketing efforts. I remember the day a previous client told me, "Stephanie, thank you for emPowering me. But I don't want to do all the marketing work. I don't have the time. Can you help me execute?"

I hadn't considered that option because *I* hadn't invested in someone helping me market my book. (Hint: We are not always our target audience.) Of course I could help, and the emPower PR Group continues to help authors in marketing execution on the regular.

SOME OF YOUR TARGET AUDIENCE WILL VALUE MONEY OVER TIME.

There was another subset of my wreath business target audience, however, who, occasionally in passing, would ask if I would ever teach them how to make one. I hadn't ever thought of that! Teaching a skill sounded interesting. It sounded fun and like a new challenge to attempt.

I was game to give the concept a try for many reasons. From a business perspective, it made financial sense as I could teach twenty people to make a wreath in the same time I could create one wreath myself. In theory, I unlocked a new opportunity to scale my business. But what excited me most was the opportunity to create with others. For me, creating is a form of therapy, and getting to create in community was something downright special.

That first workshop I held, and the others that followed, proved there was a whole group of people silently interested in my business offerings, but were unsure about the financial investment in buying one of my creations. That group, instead, were willing to invest time in *learning* the skill. This subset of my target audience valued money (and the investment they made with it) over time (as they were willing to take the time to learn something they would likely use again).

I embraced this knowledge in my own business, creating offerings in our service lineup to support authors who, too, value money over time in this way. They can get all the emPactful information for them to roll up their sleeves and tackle.

AUTHORPRENEURS SHOULDN'T LEAVE OPPORTUNITY ON THE TABLE.

Every niche—or target audience subset—has sub-niches. The perspectives of each of the subsets of my wreath business' target audience—and how they valued time and money—has legs in any and all businesses. In fact, I've actually built my own business around the same concepts my wreath business was built upon.

As you contemplate how to engage and market to your target audience, reflect on these key questions. You may be surprised what they could stir up.

Do you know the wants and needs of your target audience?

Or, prior to that question, do you have clarity on who your target audience is? Understanding who needs your offerings—whether it's your book or a derivative offering of your book's message—will help you understand if you are currently meeting the wants and needs of those individuals.

Take a deeper look at your target audience.

When you lift up the façade, you are likely to see various subsets within your target audience that have differing—and sometimes opposing—feelings, emotions, needs and wants. Some are willing to invest in your product or service while others may want to but are fearful of the investment. Understanding how they think and feel can help you move from merely marketing your business (or your book) to marketing a solution to a problem they face.

Consider how you can take your book, your business or your message and adapt it for your various audience subsets.

I'm not proposing you create so many variations of your business offerings that you find yourself spinning out of control. Instead, may I suggest you look at what you do offer and figure out if there are other opportunities to engage with those who want to work with you but may want to do it a bit differently.

In any business, it's important to focus on doing what you love to do and doing what others will invest in. But many times, we don't realize there may be a compromise—possibly something you didn't even consider becomes a new thing you love and helps you reach a group of people who would never have considered investing in you otherwise.

From my experience in nonprofit marketing (which helped plant the seeds to my marketing career), I learned firsthand that when a potential client, customer, volunteer or donor says *no* to an opportunity, it doesn't always mean *no* forever. It typically means *no* for right now. When the timing is right and the investment is worth it, that original *no* may evolve into a resounding yes.

This mindset shift in my wreath business helped me make or teach others to make over a thousand wreaths in the course of two years! My reach extended, my business grew and I uncovered a love for emPowering people with knowledge they may not have known they wanted but were pumped to have.

If you want to sell more books, build a sustainable business from your books' message and/or leverage a book as a tool for growth, take a hard look at your target audience and ask yourself, "How can I make a solution for those who value time over money *and* those who value money over time?"

---

emPowered Thoughts

How are you serving those who value time over money? These people value their time immensely and are willing to invest in solutions to their problems. How can your authorpreneur offering be a solution for them?

How are you serving those who value money over time? Money doesn't grow on trees, and these people know it. They cherish each dollar, but they also invest in value. How can you create an offering that still creates a solution in their life and one that helps you build or grow your business?

CHAPTER 19
THE BARE ROOTS OF YOUR BUSINESS

With a chai tea in one hand and a handful of dirt in the other, it was time to take a stab at the eyesore in the room and not neglect it any longer. Who knew that a Saturday morning would be the perfect conditions for a two-in-one gardening and marketing lesson!?

I couldn't overlook the twice-used plastic grocery bag for one more second. The fifty bare-root strawberry plants housed in the bag weren't going to grow legs—roots possibly, but definitely not legs—and immerse themselves into the soil. If I were to have any chance of tasting the freshness of their homegrown sweetness in the thick of the summer's heat, I had to face the challenge head on and figure out how in the world to wake them up.

Gardening has always been a favorite pastime of mine. There's nothing better than going out back and literally picking dinner for this vegetarian. For years, our family has grown a garden, and while I had learned a lot about how to perfect the hobby, I had always tackled my endeavors through the path of least resistance.

DON'T BREAK WHAT ISN'T BROKEN. IF IT WORKED LAST YEAR, IT WILL WORK AGAIN THIS YEAR.

Many of us take that same approach in business, right? How many times have you stopped before you started? Have you told yourself no on a new opportunity just because the old way worked good enough? Have you ever embraced stripping down your efforts to the bare roots and trying something different?

I had grown radishes from seeds and tomatoes from plant starters, but I had never ventured into growing plants from "bare roots." This was uncharted territory. But if I wanted to grow a strawberry patch, the bare root transplant approach was not only the most cost effective, but it was the most readily accessible.

I opened the bag of what looked like two handfuls of weeds and questioned what I had signed up for. Everything looked utterly and completely dead. I saw two withered strawberry leaves, but the rest of the piles were pathetic looking twigs and roots that appeared to have little hope. Starting something that you feel is a lost cause can be demotivating—and that's exactly where I had found myself.

I trusted my gardening skills, however, and decided to watch the video on how to plant bare-root strawberry transplants to learn more. Within ten minutes, an avid gardener explained why many plant distributors sell bare-root plants and gave me the step-by-step process on how to, in essence, wake up my strawberries. By attentively listening, I walked away with some authorpreneur advice as well (and maybe you will too)!

WHEN YOU TAKE IT TO THE ROOT, YOU ARE LESS LIKELY TO HAVE HITCHHIKERS.

A bare-root plant is one a gardener grows, and before selling, they uproot it in its dormant state, wash all of the soil off of the roots, and ship them to those who are interested. While the plants themselves look rough in this stage, there are several reasons why it makes the most sense to transport plants this way.

It's cost-effective and easier to ship. Soil is heavy, and trying to ship green plants can be cumbersome. Bare root plants are extremely light, and thus, better on the wallet. The packaging process doesn't require much, helping ensure the person selling the plants and the person purchasing them both come out winners!

You are less likely to have hitchhikers. The only hitchhikers I knew of are those I've already been taught to not pick up. But hitchhikers are also a word used for invasive plants that hitch a ride on whatever plant you are purposefully shipping. As a home gardener, I have enough trouble with weeds; I definitely don't need new invasive plants invading my garden!

After better understanding the purpose of bare-root strawberries, I opened the bag and examined what appeared to be crumbling potential.

IS IT DEAD OR MERELY DORMANT?

A year prior, I had purchased what I now know were bare-root strawberries from a local store. When I settled back home and exposed the bag of promise, I was deflated. All I saw was a bag of weird roots and soil particles. I tossed them in the garbage immediately, and simultaneously also tossed away my hope for juicy strawberries that year.

Sadly, I tossed away a bag full of potential. Bare-root strawberries, while appearing dead, are merely dormant. They have been uprooted during a time of hibernation, and once they awaken, they can bear amazing life! As with most things, the best way to wake something up is to give it a bath. Literally. And I was determined that this round of bare-root strawberries I purchased were going to be given a good faith effort.

I filled up an oversized bowl of lukewarm water and submerged my bare-root strawberries, allowing them to feel the warmth on their roots and offer a gentle reminder that they can't stay asleep forever. They had a purpose. I had a goal. Together we were going to make magic.

Under the dirt was new root growth and on each and every bare-root plant was a tiny green strawberry leaf at the crown peeking through, ready to kick it into high gear. What appeared to be dead was merely dormant, and all they needed was a little trust, a warm bath to wake up and a healthy dose of patience.[1]

YOUR AUTHORPRENEUR BUSINESS MAY BE LIKE A BARE ROOT STRAWBERRY PLANT.

Isn't that something we all need in business—and life? A little trust, a hot shower to get us started and a side of patience to allow everything to evolve as it should. In fact, you can learn a lot about your authorpreneur business and marketing strategies from a bare-root strawberry plant.

Is your idea dead or merely dormant?

I sat on the sidelines of a chlorine-filled room reflecting while my kids were in swim lessons. When my brain has an idea, whether or not the timing is right, I must find a way to capture it. I jotted down pages and pages of business ideas on how to reach a niche of my target market, and I left with a plan on how to make it happen. The next week, the pandemic hit and seemingly shattered it.

However, as I woke up my bare-root strawberries, I realized the seed of an idea that had been placed within me wasn't dead, but merely dormant. In fact, the longer that it remained dormant, the longer I had to put my business systems in place and continue to grow my audience. The idea still had merit and potential, and now the timing was right to resurrect it!

How can you take it down to the root?

It's easy for your business to evolve into something you had never planned for it to become… if you let it. Your readers and clients have new needs you try to support and outside influencers can layer on expectations that weigh you down. Before you know it, the business you envisioned starting and the one you did are two different businesses altogether. You may see this evolution as exciting. But sometimes it leads you down a path you didn't want to take.

Like the strawberry grower, how can you take your business ideas down to the root, dusting off the excess soil, giving it a wash and evaluating the purpose of your business and the offshoots from that purpose? If you focus on your purpose—your goals and your vision—first, your growth will be aligned with where *you* want to go. Sometimes, the best way to figure that out is to take it down to the root.

What hitchhikers do you need to leave behind?

We all have them—our invasive and unproductive thoughts toward our business.

- Why would anyone want to work with you?
- Why would someone choose your product over another?
- What makes you and your business worthy or worth it?

You see other businesses and begin to question your own, causing you to lose confidence or be held back from innovative opportunities. Much like the grower who finds financial value in taking strawberry plants to bare root to eliminate hitchhikers, when you take your seed of an idea, your blooming business or your new opportunity down to the root, you should harness the potential and leave behind the hitchhiker negative thoughts. Imposter syndrome isn't a healthy condition for growth. Instead, it hinders it. Leave it behind and make a pact with yourself to not pick it up.

YOUR BUSINESS IS MORE SIMILAR TO A BARE-ROOT STRAWBERRY PLANT THAN YOU THINK.

Whether you choose to leverage your book to build or grow a business that involves you working one-on-one with clients, providing tangible or intangible services or products or inspiring action through an evergreen approach, your business is similar to a bare-root strawberry plant filled with the promise of annual sweetness.

In the days where you feel exhausted and unproductive—the days where you question if your business is even going to make it—remember that sometimes dead and dormant appear alike. The only difference is what you do with the potential under the soil.

During the times when you feel heavy from your own hitchhiker thoughts, remember you don't have to pick them up. You can leave them on the sidelines or kick them to the curb. There is no need for an invasive effort to take over if it isn't going to propel you forward.

When you find yourself overwhelmed, overworked and beyond stressed, take a pause to shake off the excess soil and run yourself a warm shower. Rinse off the stuff you don't need and take a look at the bare roots. When you do, you'll find new and innovative offshoots that align with who you are and where you are destined to go next.

Building or growing a business isn't easy, but you reap what you sow. Sometimes, you'll be caking on the manure to rejuvenate the soil (yes, this is something we do annually to our garden). Other times, you will plant a seed that just won't take no matter how much care you offer it. In the end, you will see the fruits of your labor. Literally. And your author emPact will be tangible and profitable.

---

emPowered Thoughts

Is your business idea dead or dormant? The two may appear similar but are completely different. If you have a business idea but haven't given it nourishment, you could be holding on to a dormant opportunity awaiting some TLC.

What hitchhikers could you leave behind? Nearly every author—and every authorpreneur—battles imposter syndrome. I promise. Our own mental thoughts about our potential are unwanted hitchhikers we pick up without knowing. The first step in leaving them behind is uncovering them. What is holding you back most?

Take your business to the bare root. Dust off the dirt and all of the extras you've added to it (or are considering doing so). Examine your *why* and sit with your purpose. Then reevaluate if your offerings are serving both effectively. In doing so, you may uncover expenses you don't need and—better yet—new opportunities to try!

---

1. I don't know about you, but it sounds like strawberries must be my distant cousins.

CHAPTER 20
A BRISK WALK IN THE PARK

When I was a junior in college, my dad and I had a chat about his travels around the world. He was in the Navy as a young adult, and, outside of being green most days from unanticipated motion sickness, he loved traveling the world while serving his country.

He visited many countries during his tour. He soaked in the rich history in Greece and even hitchhiked through Europe once. His love for travel continued with me as together we've seen many parts of North America. But there was one country he had always wanted to visit but never had: Australia.

I could see the wonder in his eyes diminish as he spoke of visiting a country he suspected he would never have the opportunity to. Until I posed an opportunity. I had a year left in college. I could save up, he could save up and together we could explore Australia upon my graduation.

He was excited.
I was too.
Together we planned the trip of a lifetime.

LET'S PICK EXCURSIONS WITH ONLY BRISK WALKS REQUIRED.

We held open a tourist book filled with endless opportunities for exploring the land down under. There were so many choices, so little time. So my dad made a request. "Any excursion that requires more than a brisk walk, is out of the picture."

No long hikes or difficult terrain would make the list. Only brisk walks allowed (and yes, that was literally written in our tourism booklet). I shook my head, knowing my dad and his love for relaxation (and my love for a more strenuous challenge). But his rationalization had merit, and it has immense relevance when referencing authors, books and authorpreneur businesses.

An amazing ten-day trip up and down the east coast of Australia filled with nothing more than brisk walks proved the following:

- You can't soak up the moment when you are going fast. We could run through our trip, or we could savor each opportunity. We chose the latter, and I'm glad we did.
- There were so many beautiful but seemingly small moments on the trip that we would have missed if we hadn't slowed our pace. Like falling in love with dragon fruit when our tour paused at a roadside farmer's market (which is also where my dad ate the butts of green ants… Yes, that's a thing!).
- Ongoing movement in an unknown country is exhausting in and of itself. I can't imagine if it was coupled with hours of hiking trails and anything more than a brisk walk. I slept hard each night.

When building an authorpreneur business—and selecting the marketing efforts to align—leave running to the Olympic athletes and hiking to the outdoor fanatics. Instead, opt for a brisk walk any day. Here's my take on why:

- When you run a business in overdrive, you will burn out. There is not much to do when that happens outside of a CEO

- retreat, a day at the spa and prayers for rejuvenated motivation.
- If you move at laser speed, you will miss the small moments filled with beautiful successes and key learning opportunities. The listening successful authorpreneurship requires happens in the silence. It's hard to find silence if you don't create room for it.
- Exhaustion is real when you are building and growing a business no matter how fast or slow you go. Creating room for necessary breathers allows you to remain methodical and customer-centric which is where the greatest payoff happens.

If a brisk walk is the way to go, why does our culture tell you differently? Every message we consume daily shouts *buy now... take action today... don't wait*! The goal of marketing is an immediate conversion. While I know all of the tools of the trade that align with this culture-wide perspective, it's not what I believe will create sustainable businesses that have ongoing momentum.

Those businesses opt for the brisk walks in the park instead. After clarifying their offerings—and aligning them with the needs of those who are willing to invest in them—they focus on movement, consistency and efficiency.

JUST KEEP SWIMMING.

My favorite movie of all time, hands down, is the Pixar film, *Finding Nemo*. As with most animated movies, it's filled with as much goodness for adults as it is for children. Each and every time I watch it, I'm left smiling... and singing these three words on repeat.

I knew my love for the movie was a bit overkill when one of my staff members gifted me a stuffed animal version of my favorite character, Dory. My kids were too young to even cuddle the blue tang fish, but it wasn't meant for them. It was a visual reminder—nestled on the top of my file cabinet next to an inch or two of dust—of my favorite quote from the flick.

Just keep swimming.

I was known to belt out the rather catchy lyric during a meeting where we were all feeling a bit underwater from our workload. I couldn't change the expectations of us, but I could shift our focus to what we could do about it. Maybe it will be a poignant reminder for you to do the same.

Creating a business is anything but easy. Keeping the business afloat feels like you are on a ship with a leak, unable to be found. Some days, you feel like you are constantly filling buckets of water, tossing them off the ship in hopes to continue to your destination. Other times, you feel like you want to give up.

No matter your industry, business type, goals or success metrics, there is a single constant thread woven throughout. What people see and what is really happening isn't always in alignment. Embrace the iceberg, and never forget to just keep swimming.

The key to any authorpreneur's success is consistency. Notice I didn't say five social media posts a week or a thousand book sales a month. I didn't mention a revenue benchmark or a target number of clients.

Consistency is what matters.
Consistency will pay off.
Consistency separates you—an authorpreneur who will thrive—from others who may decide swimming just isn't for them.

If you keep swimming, you are consistent. You choose the pace. You choose the goals. You choose the metrics. All I ask is that you don't stop swimming. Over time, you will strengthen your once weak arms and legs and have a strong foundation that requires less doggy paddling and more backstrokes.

FAILURE IS INEVITABLE, SO FAIL FORWARD.

Social media filters have been proclaimed to solve the world's problems when it comes to hiding blemishes, but nothing can hide the fact that you are going to make a mistake in life. At least one! (And likely countless.) You're human. It's inevitable. No amount of marathon training will help you run from it.

If you can't outrun or outthink failure, the only logical option is to embrace it.

I've experienced more moments of failure than I have fingers to count, and many I would rather not relive. Some have been public and others only I've had the pleasure of seeing. Either way, they feel like speed bumps to this authorpreneur's momentum. I've wanted to run away to Hawaii and change my name. I've questioned why I've taken on the weight of business ownership. I've had sleepless nights and worry has plagued me. (Sounds like the perfect brochure for creating a business, right?!)

But I continue because I have uncovered the secret of failure.
Ready for it?

Failure is only failure if you fall backward… if you stop what you are doing altogether. Failure isn't failure if you fall forward. When that happens, failure changes its name to a much more productive one: learning.

The best learning for any business owner comes when they have a moment of setback. It's not the failure itself that matters but what direction you fall from it afterward. If you fall forward, you use your failure as an opportunity to reflect on what you could do differently next time and grow from it.

Failing forward is filled with potential.
Failing backward robs you of it.

Forward movement is just as important as consistency in any authorpreneur business. Constant refinement may occur, but ongoing learning and listening sets apart any successful business.

WORK SMARTER, NOT HARDER.

Habits are little micro movements we do over time so our brain realizes, "Hey, if I keep doing this, I'll get the results that I'm craving." Our brain turns these habits into our daily actions and, without us knowing it, we have a routine that keeps us moving toward our goals.

- For instance, I am prone to cavities (Ugh! Not fair.). I have the healthy habit of brushing my teeth twice a day and flossing. Go me!
- I've created a habit of reading. (Another healthy habit, in my humble opinion.) I have found I can't blow dry my hair in the morning if I don't have a book in front of me to read at the same time. Call this girl the queen of multitasking!
- Some habits I have aren't as commendable. For instance, when I open my phone, I have the immediate habit of checking my social media notifications. I don't even know I'm doing it. But, alas, regularly throughout the day I'm checking. This is a habit worth breaking.

Some habits you want to break free from, while others create freedom. Marketing habits built within your business can help you and your authorpreneur business work smarter, not harder. If used methodically, habits are brilliant additions to our business efforts, especially our marketing strategies and tactics. Let me explain with an example.

As I prepare for an upcoming speaking engagement, I review my content and identify marketing tactics to ensure I'm delivering A+ content in a way that provides immense value. I have an effective system in place that provides a free downloadable to align with my speaking topic and build my email list and client database at the same time. It's not salesy. It's not pushy. It's all value-add focused. And it works.

This system has become a habit in my business. I know the specific steps to set up the system. I know the content I need to build it (and many times I'm able to leverage content I already have). I know the email nurture sequence that works best. Because this has become a habit in how I prepare for my speaking engagements, it gives me freedom to focus on other efforts in my business—from client work to collaborations to new opportunities and ideas.

Habits can pertain to book marketing efforts too. In fact, they are not only baked into my own authorpreneur processes, but they are a part of how I coach nonfiction authors and authorpreneurs to work smarter, not harder. Here are a few ways you can incorporate marketing habits —and automations—to help you be more effective and efficient.

- Create a cadence for inbound marketing efforts that include providing immense value to your target audience and readers. One way I do this is through content creation. Identifying and sticking to a content creation strategy—both in creating the content, sharing the content and promoting the content—is important![1]
- Set up automated marketing systems—whether it's for social media posting, email nurturing or others—to allow your marketing to work *for* you and not the other way around. This habit makes life easier and still allows you to create the visibility efforts you are seeking.[2]
- Relationship marketing is all about follow-up, engagement and meaningful interactions. I'm a huge believer in setting up systems to support relationship marketing, and over time these efforts become habits! What you do after you are on a podcast or a media interview has the power to set you up for even more marketing success![3]
- Time batching, key messaging development, standard operating procedures (SOPs), best practices and more become standard in the work I do with authors and in their authorpreneur efforts too. These may take time to turn into habits, but once they do… oh my! Great things come from them![4]

When you think about habits, don't gloss over them as annoying behaviors you can't seem to break free from (nail biters, I see you!). Instead, see them as opportunities to create meaningful patterns in your professional life. When you embrace healthy marketing habits, you can turn what may have overwhelmed you before into what just very well may set you apart from your competition!

BUSINESS ISN'T ALWAYS A WALK IN THE PARK, BUT YOURS COULD BE A BRISK WALK THERE.

Business isn't easy, but many times the complicated parts of it were created likely by you. I say this from personal experience. It's not a cake walk by any stretch of the imagination, but you can control its pace and its success.

Like my dad, opt for brisk walks versus major hikes. Don't take on more than you can handle, and when you do (because inevitably, it will happen) learn by failing forward and growing from there. Movement matters most, and welcome opportunities for simplicity, meaningful automations or efficiencies with open arms.

You can still enjoy the benefits of a booming authorpreneur business when you take a stroll instead of a run (and, in my opinion, it's more enjoyable that way).

---

emPowered Thoughts

If you have embraced authorpreneurship and already have a growing business, reflect on the following:

What are you doing that can be done more efficiently? We all do things that bottleneck or could be done better. Don't stand in your own way. Identify them and create a plan to adapt.

**How can you slow your speed to a brisk walk versus a tireless run? Have you found yourself on the hamster wheel to nowhere? You can get off anytime and adjust your pace. Society won't tell you that, but I will.

What do you need to help keep your head above water and maintain momentum? Your feet can get tired from treading water, so remember you don't have to tackle business alone. Ask for help before you wave your white flag of surrender.

Reflection is the beginning of all learning, and taking time to reflect on the business you have will help you create the business you want.

If you know authorpreneurship is in your deck of cards but you haven't dived in yet, reflect on the following:

What parts of business excite you and what parts feel overwhelming? If you can outsource the elements that aren't in your wheelhouse, you'll have more focused time to do what only you do best.

What is your next best move? Business is a game of chess with no real rules and lots of unforeseen moves to make. In my humble opinion, the next best move is the one you are willing to make. Ongoing, consistent movement is the name of the game. Not sure where to go? My simple answer is to merely move!

What do you not know that you need to know? Well, if you knew, wouldn't you have figured it out by now? There are so many marketing aspects to building and running a business, and you don't know many until you find out that you need them. A tip to consider is to connect with experts in the industry and absorb their insights for you to consider applying. Find a trusted source of information, and follow them.

---

1. If you'd like some direction on creating a content marketing strategy, I've got you covered. Check out the emPower PR Group YouTube channel for ideas.

2. A motto of mine is "test before you invest." Before diving into paid options, take advantage of free social media schedulers, email management systems and any other marketing tools to ensure it's the best one for you before investing in it.
3. Consider what you'd *like* to do versus what you *do*. What are the differences and how can you create a system to remind you of the steps you really want to be taking but usually forget about?
4. If you haven't a clue where to start on any of these, reach out. Let's talk about your next right step. Reach out to schedule a time to chat.

PART FIVE
EMPOWERED AUTHORS LEAVE AN EMPACT

emPowered author (n): an individual who shares their emPowering message through a book as a tool to emPower others

CHAPTER 21
EMPOWER WITH A CAPITAL P

People come in and out of your life for a reason and a season. Some are a mere breath, around for a time but enriching all the same. Others are permanent fixtures, leaving a lasting impression on the makeup of who you are.

Some people you'll always remember.
Others you'll never forget.
Marie is one of those people.

The two of us began our working relationship virtually. We were on the same team. We collaborated on the same projects. Quickly we questioned if we were the same person. Outside of our accents and opposing tendency for introversion or extroversion, we could have been cut from the same cloth. We are incredibly similar. We both have dark hair and deep eyes that rest behind similar spectacles. We are about the same height on the outside, and on the inside, we tend to navigate similar worries. We were destined to be more than coworkers. Best-friendship status was a quick requirement for the two of us, and it would be the basis of our working collaboration; one that I've never experienced since.

NOTHING WAS IMPOSSIBLE WHEN THE TWO OF US TACKLED IT TOGETHER.

We had large responsibilities to handle, but no weight is too heavy to carry when it was shared. We made it through large priority projects, as well as personal ones, including maternity leave. Marie picked up my slack not once but twice during the births of my youngest two rascals.

We worked hard and also valued the importance of our mindsets, always setting time aside for some decompression and recalibration. During those moments, we would daydream about the future together.

Marie had a dream to write a book. I did not.
Marie had a dream to form a business. I did not.
But I enjoyed hearing her dreams and sharing mine alongside.

One afternoon, I sat on my plush basement couch, a welcomed retreat within my home office for daydreaming moments, as we pondered what it could look like for us to create a business together. No red tape allowed in our business. It would be filled with opportunity and strategy, two things we both loved. The concept was exciting to her and terrifying to me as we considered the what-ifs together. These moments reminded us we had control of our destiny during times control felt far off.

"If we were to form a business, Marie, what would we call it?"

It was a question I asked her regularly because her creative juices were more on point than mine. We brainstormed many names, but all fell flat until a peer of ours made a comment about what happens when the two of us come together. "Power," he noted. From that point on, he called us the power twins. Power had to be the basis of a business name for us one day.

The layoff that changed the trajectory of my life also changed hers. We were both impacted by it, and it was because of our friendship we both made it through those stressful moments of tension and fear. Moments when I was at rock bottom, she wasn't and would extend a virtual hand to lift me up. Times when she fretted about the future, I was grounded in the present and would invite her there with me. Together, we supported each other as we navigated our new normal.

She applied for jobs and, of course, was snatched up when a great opportunity presented itself. I, on the other hand, had accepted her challenge to write a blog, which led to me publishing a book. I never planned on writing one; she did. Yet, it turned into a gateway for me to form a business. It wasn't on my radar, but Life changed course and, when it did, Marie was cheering me on from the sidelines.

BEFORE THE EMPOWER PR GROUP WAS FORMALLY IN PLACE, AUTHORS FOUND *ME*.

They needed help. I offered solutions. They saw I could help them, and they didn't take no for an answer. I've always been someone who wants to help, and when it was time to put a name to the business, I knew it needed to be a part of it. But this marketing guru has learned it is easier to help others than it is to help oneself. I hadn't a clue what to call my business, but I needed to figure it out and pronto.

I was driving down the road, tuning out the chaos of the backseat where my children were perched watching a movie and likely in the throes of a sibling fight, when it came. A wave of inspiration. I knew the name of the business I had been forming, and it stemmed from my collaboration with Marie.

When I reflected back on how the two of us collaborated, our outcomes were powerful and impactful, not for any other reason than we knew together we could make something out of nothing. Power was how we propelled our work forward; emPowering is what we did in the process. I realized that's the essence of what I do, of what emPactful authors do.

Choice is always at your fingertips, like writing a book to build or grow a business or reading a book and taking action from it. Choice is always within our control, even when our life feels like it's spinning out of it.

The emPower PR Group was born out of the goal to emPower authors to emPower others. But it was formed when I was emPowered by a dear friend who pushed me to write a blog, even when I believed wholeheartedly there was nothing of substance there. It was chiseled from a friendship that believed anything was possible and that, together, we could conquer any mountain.

ALWAYS CAPITALIZE THE P IN EMPOWER.

Authors have stories. They write books. They share them with their readers. They build businesses from them too. But emPowered authors pivot how they see their craft and realize they have an opportunity very few have.

EmPowered authors know the book is merely a communication vessel tasked with changing lives along the way. EmPowered authors become emPowered themselves so they can propel their message forward in the hopes of changing lives in the process. EmPowered authors don't see their work finished when the book is published. They see it as the beginning of something big, something meaningful, something emPowering and emPactful.

EmPowered authors know their purpose in life is to emPower others. The capital P in emPower is in honor of those who believed in you—just like Marie believed in me—and a constant reminder that you matter, your message matters and your book matters too.

You are an emPowered author. And, in case you could use the boost of confidence, know that I believe in you!

---

emPowered Thoughts

Who in your life is your capital P? EmPowered people have been emPowered themselves. Reflecting on those who built you up will help you inspire future generations. Take a moment to do so.

EmPowerment isn't a privilege; it's an honor. As you reflect on your marketable book (or the one you are going to write), your charge to share your message (and sell books) and your calling to build or grow a business alongside (your invitation to become an authorpreneur) remember the honor authors are given and never take it for granted. How can you emPower others?

CHAPTER 22
DON'T THINK DIFFERENTLY, THINK DIFFERENT

No one could have predicted it coming. Truly. It was as if out of thin air what we all knew to be normal was turned upside down in every way. What people dubbed "The Great Lockdown" was the beginning of a pandemic that changed lives and businesses in ways no one could have imagined.

I remember the day the COVID pandemic chaos seeped into my life. I had a virtual webinar for a business development cohort I was a part of, and a sales expert was invited to inspire us on new ways to reach new people. This expert was secured well in advance, prior to schools and businesses closing, but boy was her offering relevant.

Out of all of her amazing thoughts and tailored suggestions, I will never forget one phrase she tossed out for us to ponder. Then we went around the virtual classroom to react to her statement.

"THIS IS A TIME TO NO LONGER THINK DIFFERENTLY, BUT RATHER, TO THINK DIFFERENT."

She was curious what that statement meant to each of us in our current lives and in our current businesses. I gave it some time to sink in, and when she asked my thoughts, I knew exactly what it meant and what I was charged to do next.

When you think differently, you are thinking outside of the box you currently work within. Your area of expertise is in the box, but you see new extensions and derivative works to support your current box's business. That's thinking differently.

But thinking different? Well, you pick up your normal box and put it in the closet, saving it for later. You compartmentalize that box, knowing that one day you can bring it out again. But now you create a whole new box, looking at your expertise and your business in new ways altogether. You start thinking differently—creating new extensions and derivatives of your work again—about your think different box.

By the end of the call, I had an entire whiteboard full of think different opportunities for my current clients and my business altogether. This new approach was meant to help each of us be prepared to rebound when the world would come back to normal instead of needing to rebuild our business altogether. What a brilliant concept.

HOW CAN YOU THINK DIFFERENT ABOUT YOUR BOOK AND YOUR AUTHORPRENEUR BUSINESS?

I don't know about you, but I've never fit inside of a box. The way I think and work is too big and too broad to be wrapped in paper and topped with a bow.

The pandemic is an experience no one wants to relive. There are more negative outcomes than I could ever list, but I am always looking for silver linings if and when possible. The status quo no longer mattered. Typical "boxes" of how things always worked, no longer worked. Income was stretched, worries surmounted and yet I helped many authors write marketable books and launched them successfully during that trying time.

How? We put away the old way of doing things and pulled out cardboard to create brand new boxes from scratch.

While a pandemic may never impact our lives again like it did during COVID, no one is safe from change. No author. No business. No one. Successful authors and authorpreneurs expect it and are flexible enough to work through it.

Want some tips to help you craft your own think different box? Here are some of my favorites.

- Ask for feedback, and be receptive to it. Editorial boards and beta readers give insights into how your book will be received before publishing.
- Watch for trends on how people consume information. How can your book or business align with them? Better question, how can you create one?
- Know and understand the people who need what you have to offer. You are likely not your target reader, so do your research.
- Keep your creative juices flowing. Know where you need to go to step out of your box. For me, it could be a weekend retreat to the mountains. Take time to unplug and recharge because many times you hold the answers.
- Change can be scary, intimidating even. Start small and test. Unless you are an aircraft engineer, take my advice and build the plane while flying it. See if someone will bite at your think different idea before investing too much time into it.

Don't let change be a reason to stop your momentum—whether that's in launching a book, growing your business or doing both.

If you lead with value, success will follow. Pull out your new think different box, build upon the expertise you bring to all who can benefit from your work and continue to focus on value first!

It will pay off.

Honestly, you may find you like your new "box" better anyway!

---

emPowered Thoughts

How is your "box" working for you? If you are a first-time author, you may not even know what your box looks like yet. Or, if you have written a book in a niche market, your box may forever be sufficient. Don't fix what isn't broken. But don't overlook the opportunity to think differently or different altogether.

CHAPTER 23
BE THE TORTOISE NOT THE HARE

I have always loved animals. Nowadays, most call me the cat whisperer, but I attract anything with fur or feathers or critters who make squeaky sounds. (And mosquitos, but those I don't welcome.)

I always wanted to own a cat… a dog, even… but my dad's constant struggle of managing an indoor pet didn't allow for a life-long companion until I was fifteen. Prior to then, my parents appeased my need for animal cuddles with more atypical options.

I had plenty of fish. Betta fish were my favorites. Before I was figuratively running on hamster wheels, I would watch the countless ones I adopted run on their own. I had a bird named Tweety after my favorite Looney Tunes character. But my most memorable and unexpected fluffy companion was my bunny, Snuggles.

Snuggles was a small, short-haired ball of sweetness. She was gray as coal and had a white tail that looked like a single, massive cotton ball. Her nose was constantly moving as she took in the smells of her surroundings. She was loving.

While I was grateful for her wonderful attributes, she had plenty others that no one told me about before we invited her into our home… like her toe nails. If you didn't trim them regularly, they would grow and twist, making it hard for her to hop. Cats and dogs have nails, but regular vet visits account for keeping them in shape. A fly might have surely thought they were attending a comedy show when my mom and I would have to clip her nails.

Rabbits also stink (like really, really, really badly). Nowadays, I have five indoor cats, and no amount of litter box odor compares to that of a rabbit. I'm sure my parents regretted the decision to have a pet rabbit, but I never did. I loved Snuggles tremendously.

SHE WAS SMART. SHE WAS PURPOSEFUL. SHE WAS FAST. IN RETROSPECT, SHE AND I HAD A LOT IN COMMON.

I move through life at high speed if I'm not careful. Ask anyone who spends an hour with me, and they will testify to the haste with which I move through life. (It's great for my clients; it's exhausting for me!) I am fueled by the need for speed, which is why I got a speeding ticket every year of my driving life from sixteen to twenty.

Even though I am from the South, a slow pace frustrates me. I want to do all the things and I want to do them right now.[1] Now. Not tomorrow. I have things to do, people to help, books to write and places to go. Time feels limited to me, and the opportunities appear endless. I want to conquer them all.

I am much like Snuggles… a bunny, or rather, a hare.

As I would read my children the fable of the tortoise and the hare, I always identified with the latter most. How can we get to our end goal in the most effective and efficient way… and the quickest? As a young adult, I thought the only way to do so was alone. Others slowed me down and were uncontrollable. In school, I opted for self-led projects versus group ones, because group efforts irritated me (and inevitably, I'd do all the work anyway).

You would expect this hare to love the fast pace of marketing, yet, even this gal who has a need for speed realizes the importance of pace. In marketing efforts, I also have to remind myself to slow down because the rush of others isn't sustainable. It's not even possible. It's overwhelming. Unless you are up for learning something new every five seconds (because that's how quickly it feels like this industry shifts), even the fastest hare can't get it all done.

The beautiful truth is you don't have to.

I GREW UP ALWAYS WANTING TO LIVE ON A FARM.

My grandparents had a farm we frequented. My dad and I would pack a bag of necessities and travel to the middle of nowhere most weekends of my childhood. That farm was where I learned how to garden and take care of cows. It's where I learned why you wear gloves when handling untreated wood. (Splinters are the worst, even if you get them going up to rest in the treehouse.) It's where I learned how to be aware of ticks before they are aware of you, and before they decide to take residence in your scalp. It's where I learned how to fish and hike. How to pour your heart and soul into God's green earth. How to work hard and eat well. How love is measured not by things but by moments.

It's also where I found an appreciation for the turtles. Not the snapping kind but the box version.

Life is a bit slower in the country where there is no cell service and there's nothing on television except for the old movies my grandpa had collected over the years. When my dad and I would leave the city to trek to the farm, it didn't matter the speed on our speedometer because the pace of life slowed nonetheless.

The best conversations occurred in the evenings around our outdoor fire my grandma would poke to keep alive. Sweat seeped from our pores, but we slept well and ate even better. Picking the food you had for dinner was special and delicious. Life was simple but meaningful, and every adventure always had a turtle encounter or two.

Inevitably, the turtle would decide the journey across the road was an important one to do before we would drive by. Occasionally a chicken would be crossing the road, but usually it was the turtle instead. In the country, you don't fly by. You stop and help, even if the help is needed by a turtle. We would turn on the flashers, and my dad would hop out to offer aid to the turtle. Shy but grateful, the turtle would continue on its quest safely.

When my husband and I moved our family to a twenty-five acre farm years later, I found myself smiling in the warm seasons when the turtles would put themselves in precarious circumstances. Saving a turtle feels pretty amazing, if I do say so myself. Every time I do, I am reminded of the pace of my own life and the pace of my work too.

TURTLES ARE METHODICAL. THEY ARE FOCUSED. THEY DON'T GIVE UP THEIR ENERGY FOR WRONG MOVES.

Yet, they still find themselves in some situations they'd rather not be in. Even in a pickle, they remain focused on their goal and keep moving. They also welcome help… as long as they aren't snappers. Those will bite off your fingers—literally—if you offer it even though, begrudgingly, they know they need you.

In the marketing race, it feels like speed is a requirement of success. The new shiny object syndrome will do that to you. So will the comparison game. Don't let it. Period.

Most marketers align with the hare and will encourage you to as well. Quicker movements bring on quicker metrics, which should create quicker outcomes. Or, at least that's what they tout. But it's not what I have found to be true. Especially for book marketing.

Methodical movement is what converts. Trying something just because someone else did doesn't mean it's the right tactic to put your energy and resources into. It could take you on a costly detour. Instead, slow, persistent, methodical movement will always win.

Maybe the quick efforts will make you go viral today, but the methodical ones will make you stay relevant for tomorrow.

Maybe the quick efforts will help you reach the finish line before your opponent, but the methodical ones will help you cross multiple finish lines when your opponent has run out of steam.

Maybe the tortoise approach won't equate to a multitude of immediate book sales, but rather consistent and long-term sales increases. That is what will win in the end.

I thought I was a hare, and owning one is a reminder it's usually my tendency to move fast. But every time I see a turtle, I smile knowing slow and steady will always triumph, especially in the book marketing race.

---

emPowered Thoughts

Do you identify with the hare? Is your tendency to move fast? Is speed your middle name? How can you embrace your need for movement while letting go of your need for speed? In the marketing race, speed will appear triumphant, but as you know, perception isn't always reality.

How can you be more like the tortoise? Every move you make matters. Slow, methodical movement will ensure that you create a book that is emPactful and a business that is successful.

---

1. As I have shared insights with you throughout the book on pace and focus, I continue to remind myself to practice what I know works, even if it's against my initial tendency.

CHAPTER 24
WHEN YOU KNOW, YOU CAN'T UNKNOW

There are some things we should expect to become experts at over time. Take grocery shopping for instance. Most of us frequent the grocery store weekly, monthly at least, so knowing the ins and outs of where your favorite items are and where to pay for them should become common knowledge. Or, if driving is your thing, knowing the laws of the road become cemented in your subconscious.

Daily work functions, personal hygiene habits and even riding a bike are repetitive behaviors many of us learn quickly and can do on autopilot. But writing, publishing and marketing a book is usually not among them. (Even most professional authors will never publish as many books as often as they go to the grocery.)

Many people dream of writing a book but very few actually do. Those of us who do don't always know how to write a marketable one. Some write a book but never publish it. Others learn the ins and outs of the publishing industry. Even the most skilled of marketers who write books usually need help to market their own because successfully marketing a book doesn't always follow the rules of the trade.

Until I went through the process of writing my first book, I didn't understand what would make it marketable. The publishing industry is constantly evolving, and I learn more every time I publish another book of mine. Some of my best tried and true marketing tactics evolved from testing the promotion of my own books.

YOU DON'T KNOW UNTIL YOU KNOW, AND WHEN YOU KNOW YOU CAN'T UNKNOW.

What may seem like a tongue twister has become a philosophical way of life for me. Knowledge is powerful, but many times we don't know we are missing something, until we learn of it.

Consider your favorite candy. Were you missing something in life before it existed? Probably not. Now that I know Reese's Pieces are a thing, don't ever try to give me Sno-Caps. Now that I know what it's like to snorkel in the Great Barrier Reef, an afternoon outing off the coast of Florida just doesn't meet the mark. Once you know, it's hard to forget.

I have been asked by many what I wish I would have known when I was publishing my first book. What are some mistakes authors could dodge when marketing theirs? Here's a list of some things I now know and can't unknow within the industry.

UNDERSTAND WHY YOU ARE WRITING A BOOK IN THE FIRST PLACE, AND WHERE YOU WANT THE BOOK TO TAKE YOU.

How can you reach a destination without a road map? Why did you pick that destination in the first place? Understanding *why* you wrote a book will give you insight into where you want the book to take you.[1] Gaining clarity on your end goal will help you picture success.

Success varies from author to author. Knowing what that looks like for you will help you leverage the best marketing strategies and tactics to get there. This industry may encourage you to compare yourself to others but don't. Your success and another author's success will never be the same. If you feel the comparison pull, redirect that energy back to your *why*.

GAIN CLARITY ON WHO NEEDS YOUR BOOK AND HOW TO FIND THEM.

Finding your target audience is something all marketing experts will suggest. Knowing your target audience's *wants* and *needs*, and then ensuring your book meets a need of theirs is where the key differentiator takes place. Individuals are more likely to purchase a book (or a derivative offering from it) if it meets a need in their lives. Find a way for your book to not be just a want (like a fun beach read) but instead meet and become a need (this is going to be game changing for my life and pronto). This is done through effective marketing efforts to the right target audiences.[2]

If you don't know the needs of your target audience, research them. Successful books are written because someone out there *needs* to read them. If you don't have that clarity, take time to get it as early as you can in the process. It may add a few extra days, weeks or even months to your production schedule, but I can guarantee you the success of your book will be more vast when it is published.

DON'T WAIT TO DEVELOP AN AUTHOR PLATFORM; START NOW!

An author platform is just a fancy term for a place to create demand, leverage engagement, share content, outline offerings and sell books! For most, this includes a blend of a digital presence (typically a website), a social media presence (being visible and engaging on one or several social media outlets), a tool for communication (an email management system) and a visibility strategy (what you are doing to get seen and heard on an ongoing basis). Many authors wait until the book releases before building this. Don't. Do it now! You'll thank me in the long run.[3]

I have found that the scariest part of this process is just getting started. Consider this my permission for you to take the first step today. Perfection is not required, but movement is. Your readers don't want you to be anyone but *you*. Don't let overthinking the process entirely overwhelm you from connecting with them. Successful author platforms include value sharing and a lot of listening.

DON'T HINDER YOUR CONNECTIONS' ABILITY TO HELP YOU SPREAD THE WORD.

Often the hardest part of being an author (outside of writing the book itself) is telling those who know you and love you about it. Writing a book is an extremely vulnerable process, so much so that many authors dodge mentioning it to their connections. But when done right, your connections can become an army of supporters for you. Let me tell you, they want to be.

Don't let your friends, family, coworkers and peers find out about your book from anyone outside of you. In fact, invite them into the process with you. EmPower them to tell their connections about this amazing author they know and this book they *must* read. You may be one or two degrees away from someone who desperately needs your book's message and your connections may help your book find them.[4]

REALIZE THAT YOUR BOOK IS ACTUALLY THE START OF A BUSINESS.

The quicker you realize what you have to offer is more than *just* a book, the quicker you will be able to leverage the book in new and creative ways. Some of the best ways to market books are by leveraging their content to provide immersive and experiential workshops, speaking engagements and coaching and consulting support. Readers who fall in love with your message—especially if the book is nonfiction—will likely reach out wanting to know more, learn more and work with you directly. Give thought to where you want the book to take you, and if you identify that prior to the book's release, be sure to add it in the back of the book, which is prime marketing space.[5]

Think like your target audience and leverage your book and your other offerings to be solutions to their current problems. If you find that challenging, no sweat. The best skill in growing an authorpreneur business requires you to put your pen down and open your ears. If your book is the basis of a potential business, others will tell you. In fact, they may see it before you do.

YOU DON'T KNOW UNTIL YOU KNOW, AND WHEN YOU KNOW, YOU MAY FEEL AN UH-OH.

Deep sigh. If you are like most authors, there is likely something that you did in your book journey that you would have preferred to have done differently after you learned what works and what doesn't. Rest assured I've seen (and experienced) plenty of author *oops*. However, most of them are fixable. Here are a few that I see regularly that maybe I can help you avoid.

- You may be ready to be done with your book, but don't neglect the necessary steps to make sure it is a marketable one. Don't hop over the editing process, and be certain to invest in expert help when you need it. No amount of marketing can create ongoing momentum if your book isn't a marketable one.
- People judge a book by its cover. Your cover matters, and your title and subtitle do as well. Don't overlook the importance of perfecting what people will see and read first.[6] People don't buy problems; they invest in solutions. Make sure your title and cover reflect that.
- Don't fall into the social media trap by diving into building a presence on all social media platforms and end up not building a following on any. It's better to be on a few social platforms well than on all of them poorly. It's all about knowing your target reader and being where they are (and where you enjoy).
- Don't invest high dollars in the wrong marketing efforts. It hurts me to see authors have websites built that miss the mark; invest in major courses, coaches, etc. when they aren't ready; or prioritize the wrong priorities. The best way to hike up the mountain isn't to keep your eyes on the mountain top, but rather to keep your eyes on your feet. Just focus on the next right thing. Get that done well and then go to the next. Along the way, look for a guide who you trust and can help you make the right next move.[7]

Knowledge is learned. It helps you remember to clip your coupons before frequenting the grocery so you can get the best deals. It helps you arrive at a destination safely after a comfortable drive. It identifies efficiencies to make your job more enjoyable and more productive.

Knowledge also helps ensure the book you want to write will sell and reach those who need and want it most! The best part about knowledge is it is meant to be shared. Because, when you know, you can't help but tell others.

emPowered Thoughts

What is something you wish you would have known when writing, publishing and marketing your book? Hindsight is always 20/20. Looking back on your journey, what do you wish you would have known that would have made it a bit easier for you? Jot it down. (If you're comfortable, I'd like to know it too! The more I know, the more I can help others like you in the future.)

Are you in the thick of an uh-oh? Very few *uh-ohs* can't be fixed. Many *uh-ohs* are known only to you. If you're in the thick of one, take a deep breath and know you don't have to navigate it alone.

---

1. Every time you go to write a new book or evaluate your marketing strategies accordingly, invite chapter 1 back into your life. Your takeaways from it will evolve as you develop your authorpreneurship.
2. With a brownie in hand, reread chapter 6 for an audience needs boost.
3. Part 3 provides guidance on where to start and how to continue building and leveraging an author platform. If you haven't built an author platform, check out chapter 11. If you are still overwhelmed by social media, chapter 12 is a great place for you to revisit. If you find yourself getting excited about visibility efforts (or trying to run away from them), chapter 15 is your best friend.
4. If you're still a little queasy about emPowering your connections to help you, look back at chapter 14.
5. As you embrace authorpreneurship, pull out a highlighter and revisit part 4.
6. If you're looking for inspiration, check out the emPower PR Group's YouTube channel for additional thoughts.
7. Chapter 5 is a beautiful companion to your book hike, and if you need a guide, the emPower PR Group is here.

CHAPTER 25
YOUR BOOK IS NOT A BANANA

My favorite advice to give an author is the best advice I received while publishing my first book. I was one big ball of nerves filled with both pure excitement and utter terror for others to consume my memoir. I knew it was worth it, but I wasn't sure I was worthy. I knew my book would make an emPact, but I was afraid I wasn't doing enough.

Your book is not a banana.

That single-sentence piece of advice left me perplexed and with a giggle. Of course it's not a banana. You can't eat it. It doesn't grow on trees. It is not going to go bad in three days and need to be tossed.

Thank heavens my book is not a banana, even though I love them. But for whatever reason, my family of five can't seem to eat all the bananas in a bunch quick enough before it makes phone calls to the enormous family of gnats awaiting an invitation for a party on my counter. Within a few days, a banana can go from delicious to disaster. But your book won't.

It cannot be eaten, though it can be consumed.
It has no shelf life. You can breathe life into it whenever you want.
It doesn't draw gnats. It draws people and changes lives in the process.

Remembering your book is not a banana is something we all need to hear from time to time because book marketing can cause panic, especially around a book's launch.

You think you need to do *all* the things, but I like to encourage authors to consider doing *some* of the things and doing them well. Then you can invite other tactics to the conversation over time. Your book's marketing efforts should not be seen as a sprint but rather a marathon. Focused, strategic and purposeful movement over time will be more effective than a quick effort that isn't sustainable.

YOUR BOOK IS NOT A BANANA, AND YOU AREN'T EITHER.

A week or two prior to a book launch is usually when an author can no longer hide behind their mask of confidence. Nerves take over, telling them a story that usually isn't true. It's one filled with worry of what people will think. It's one filled with fear they haven't done enough. It's one filled with concern that success isn't in their book's deck of cards.

I was coaching two authors jointly on their book launch when I saw their masks crumble. They were navigating this worry alone in silos, and I knew nothing I said at that moment tactically mattered. I could give them additional advice or toss out a new strategy for consideration, but I knew it would be overlooked. That day wasn't a day for short-term marketing strategies; it was a day to fuel long-term momentum.

I pulled out my bag of tricks, and all that was left was the single most important advice I have ever received. *Your book is not a banana.* I've grown fond of seeing an author's face when I finish that sentence. Some look at me with concern. Others offer a confused smile. These two women leaned forward knowing I was about to impart a piece of wisdom that would emPower them.

Even over Zoom I saw a new glitter in their eyes as tears gathered and their shoulders lowered as they exhaled relief. No words were required for me to know their feelings because I had been there too. When I received that advice, I was grateful for the reminder that I chose the pace and that there is no shelf life on my book.

"And I'm not a banana either."

One of the women softly uttered those words. It was as if she was pouring into me as I had just poured into her. She deepened that piece of advice for me as I realized it wasn't limited to a book. Author friend, it's meant for you too.

You are not a banana.

In case you needed a reminder that you are way cooler than a delicious piece of fruit, I wanted to be the one to tell you that today. You have much life to live, to share and to give. On behalf of all of your readers —those who have read your book and those who one day will be blessed to do so—thank you for sharing you.

---

emPowered Thoughts

Now that you know your book is not a piece of fruit, let me tell you what else it is not:

Transactional. It may feel that way, but a marketable book isn't.
Every part of you. It is a part of you, but you are so much more.
The end. It's actually the beginning.

Your book and you are not a banana. Never forget that.

BOOKS BUILD BRIDGES AND BREAK DOWN WALLS

Our world, unfortunately, is a polarizing one with conflicting opinions everywhere you turn. The beauty of our uniqueness has also become reason for our differences and the heartbreak of challenges. What could unite us as different people with different perspectives—all worthy and warranted—has created a great division. And it makes my heart hurt immensely.

Walls are built daily. Figurative ones. In some places, literal ones too. Barricades are put up, closing people out of opportunity or willingness to be open-minded. Fences shut down conversation, stories, voices. Opinions and perspectives are no longer respected, and it's tough to be heard.

But when stories aren't shared, no one wins.
When people aren't valued, no one wins.
And when walls are built, no one wins too.

I am horrible at remembering inspirational quotes on demand, but when something does stick, it sticks like superglue. A message a pastor shared during a sermon at church is one of them. A simple but meaningful phrase he shared changed how I see the world, how I see myself and how I see the opportunity each author is gifted with.

WE SHOULD BE PEOPLE WHO BUILD BRIDGES AND BREAK DOWN WALLS.

When I was in high school, I traveled to France and Spain with my class for an educational trip. I was so young that the specifics of the places we visited remain vague—like the remnants of a dream—outside of the terrifying elevator ride half-way up the Eiffel Tower, a picturesque experience in Versailles and the moment our bus arrived in Toledo.

I felt like I had stepped into a photoshopped postcard when we arrived in Toledo. A city surrounded by a moat with a handful of bridges that paved a welcoming entry awaited. Walls kept in a hidden treasure, but the bridge allowed others to experience it. Without the bridge, the rich history and detailed architecture would remain in confinement, only to be appreciated by the city's community. What a shame that would be, for it was the highlight of my trip!

Walls may keep precious things safe, but hoarding holds back. Sharing is what allows growth to happen, and bridges are the tool to do just that.

Walls close out.
Bridges open up.
Walls hold back.
Bridges create connection.

Thank heavens for the bridge in Toledo. It connected everything—known to unknown, beauty to possibility. Because of the bridge, I'll always cherish my time exploring that ancient city.

And because of books, I'll always cherish my time better understanding the perspectives of others who see the world through a different lens than I do. Books build bridges and break down walls too.

YOU DON'T HAVE TO BE AN ARCHITECT TO BUILD BRIDGES. AND YOU DON'T HAVE TO KNOW HOW TO MANEUVER HEAVY MACHINERY TO BREAK DOWN WALLS.

As authors, books can accomplish our mission.

Books allow stories to be told and be heard during times when fences aren't needed and walls don't matter. In fact, books are much like light in that they can figuratively wiggle through the tiny space between fence boards. Even the closest boards can't eliminate the morning sun or the potential a book offers.

All walls aren't built from concrete, and even the ones that are don't have to be permanent. Books can slowly chisel away any man-made barrier or small-mindedness one faces by giving a glimpse into the life of another—in a raw and vulnerable way—allowing us to set aside any difference and actually hear another's perspective. And it changes people in the process.

Books are powerful. I've always known that. But I've seen just how powerful they can be. They can change our landscape—and they come equipped with sledgehammers and dynamite to break down walls in our lives. And in return, page by page they hammer nails into the bridge they slowly build in its place.

Some bridges are built from suspension cables. They are effective but flexible and could be impacted by change—or even the wind. They connect but are not yet solid.

Others are drawbridges, allowing the choice to let in another when and if they are ready. These bridges create progress and, over time, possibly the need to retract the bridge diminishes altogether.

On my family farm, we have a small but mighty bridge that connects our front acreage to the back. The front is where we live, but the back is where we yearn to be. The bridge isn't perfect, but it's solid. When the clouds unzip and flood the bridge, the concrete blocks hold strong. We continue to build onto it, even if erosion attempts to take it. We control the strength of that bridge, and you control the strength of yours too.

No matter the size, the type or even the quality of a bridge, a bridge is still a bridge, and building one has to start somewhere.

You, your message, your book and your business could be the beginning of a bridge. You are in the business of wall deconstructing and bridge construction. Your book comes equipped with the raw materials needed to begin the process, and your story is what shakes the foundation of any wall. When we layer our stories, we become interconnected and our bridges become strong.

Author friend, we aren't just writing books or sharing stories, we are changing lives. We are changing people. We are changing communities. We are changing our world. And we are changing ourselves in the process.

This is the power of each author's emPact—and it's the power of yours.

A SPECIAL GIFT FROM ME TO YOU

To make your author emPact, readers need to be able to… oh, I don't know… *buy* your book! In the publishing industry, this is called distribution. But to most authors, it means one word: Amazon.

Amazon is currently the primary platform readers frequent to purchase a book. Of course bookstores are a book lover's dream, but if you are wanting to make a large emPact, you can't neglect the importance of Amazon in your distribution and promotional efforts.

I wanted to give you a gift to help you get started!

This gift won't be delivered to your doorstep, but it is a bundle of goodness prepared just for you, my author friend. I've pulled together some Amazon insights any and all authors can benefit from so that you are privy on how to take full advantage of the platform and be sure you stick out among the vast competition.

Visit authoremPact.com to receive my gift packaged and ready for you!

NOW THAT YOU'RE EMPOWERED...

What's your next move?

Remember, I believe in strategic movement and that no one has to make movement alone. I am just a video chat away, and the programs and resources with the emPower PR Group were designed with you in mind. No matter where you are, we can help you.

- If you are an aspiring author, we can ensure that you write a marketable book.
- If you are looking to launch or relaunch your book, we are poised to support you in doing so.
- If you are looking to build or grow a business alongside your book and embrace authorpreneurship, we would be honored to become your business cheerleader.

WE AREN'T A ONE-SIZE-FITS-ALL; WE ARE A ONE-SIZE-FITS-YOU.

Every author has different needs, budgets, time restrictions, capacity and interests when it comes to book marketing. We know this and we've embraced it. We don't want to be a barrier to book success, but rather a support solution. Here are the ways that we offer help.

We are in the business of value sharing.

For authors equipped to roll up their sleeves and run with the book marketing advice we offer, be sure to check out our podcast, *The emPowered Author Podcast*, for timely marketing tips. The emPower PR Group has a robust YouTube channel offering a slew of productive rabbit holes for your viewing pleasure. We've been known to provide complimentary workshops to our email subscribers, so be sure to join our email list by visiting emPowerPRGroup.com.

We love being a complement to your team and/or efforts.

For authors who want us to roll up our sleeves, we offer done-for-you and done-with-you services.

- Our programs allow our team to deep dive into your unique needs and support you with tactical execution.
- Maybe all you need is one day or week of focused support. We offer solutions that provides our team the opportunity to fully immerse ourselves into you, your book and your message. This intensive work positions you for forward momentum.
- A lot can be accomplished in an hour. If you have a handful of pressing questions and are looking for the roadmap to accomplish them, our marketing strategy sessions may be just what you need.

WE TAKE OUR OWN ADVICE; WE ARE SUPERB LISTENERS.

Your book has legs and marketing does too. So many, actually, that you could feel like you are herding spiders. As you deepen your marketing efforts, new opportunities arise. We pride ourselves on being a team of trusted industry experts who use our skills to help you increase your emPact.

In addition to the strategy support and tactical execution we offer in our programs, the emPower PR Group also has various services to support different authors' marketing needs. From websites to branding, podcast creation to podcast pitching, photography to videography and everywhere in between, we are a one-stop book marketing solution.

LET'S CONNECT AND SEE HOW WE CAN HELP YOU!

Visit emPowerPRGroup.com to learn more about the emPower PR Group, and if you click "connect" and fill out our "help me help you" form, we will send you a link to my calendar, and we can have a free fifteen-minute chit chat. I love those calls!

If you want to learn more about me as an author, visit Stephanie-Feger.com.

I love emPowering authors, especially those who love to emPower others. Now that you're emPowered, it's your turn to pass the emPowerment baton and make your author emPact.

ACKNOWLEDGMENTS

EmPact is finicky. It's so hard to measure the emPact you make. What is easier to measure is the emPact others have made on you.

My mom and dad have always believed in me, and they've always emPowered me. I was raised to be a strong young woman with a powerful voice. (Whether they liked it or not!) Books have been a part of my emPowerment journey for as long as I can remember. Instead of Easter candy, I got Easter books and that extended to nearly every holiday. I'm grateful to the two of them for inspiring me to be whatever I wanted to be and only sometimes pushing me to go outside to play when I really wanted to be inside reading.

Learning to read didn't happen overnight, and neither did learning to write. I'm grateful to be afforded an education that believed in the power of both. While I can't remember the names of every educator who helped me perfect my craft, I'm grateful to each for pouring into me where and when I was. From a high school teacher who coordinated a book club for extra credit (even though I was acing his class and didn't need it), to a college professor who questioned the quality of a pass/fail paper, thank you for giving me the chance to see reading as an ongoing joy and the challenge to never settle with my writing.

I've been asked before who I'd like to meet when I get to heaven, and outside of my grandparents, my daughter and other loved ones, I hope to throw a Thanksgiving feast for all the authors who shaped me without knowing it. My gratitude for them runs deep. They were living proof that books change people for they have changed me.

I would have never listened to Life if Marie Thornsberry hadn't been a beacon for it. She saw in me something I didn't, and she believed I had something to say that others wouldn't just listen to but actually needed to hear. A friend like that is hard to find, and I'm grateful she is a part of my Life's tapestry.

There isn't a single idea I've had that my husband Cory has thought was crazy. (And don't worry, I've tossed out many that I even thought were out in left field.) Starting a blog, he encouraged. Writing a book, he supported. Creating a business to fund the book journey, he actively shared. Listening to God's calling in my life, he held my hand and walked with me. No one deserves to be loved as much as he loves me. I'm the woman I am today because of him.

My life's purpose changed the day I became Momma. My three changed the lens through which I see the world. Seeing life through their eyes puts everything into perspective. Eli's willingness to speak his truth inspires me to have the courage to speak mine. Lyndi's deep love for all people reminds me to focus on giving instead of receiving. Luke's ability to make a friend everywhere he goes helps me break down walls I don't even know I have. They may think that they are looking up to me, but I am the one who looks up to them. (Figuratively of course, but in a few years I will likely be the shortest of our crew!)

I have hung up my type-A personality for a rainy day, knowing good and well that day will never come. Even though I used to think I was in control of life, I never was. God is the perfect artist, choosing when to use colored pencils, charcoal or watercolor. He leads each instrument as He orchestrates my opportunities. He is the master gardener planting seeds outside my peripheral vision that constantly bear fruit I've never tasted before. He is my cheerleader and my therapist. He loves me, and He constantly proves that by bringing people and opportunity into my life.

I didn't want to write a book, but God had other plans. He helped me find the people who made it a reality. Cathy Fyock and Kate Colbert helped bring my first book to life and saw in me a skillset others needed that I could share.

I didn't want to start a business, but God had other plans. He helped me find the people to help it grow. Jessie White and Kerrigan Miller help place stepping stones so we can emPower more authors.

I didn't want to build a team, but God had other plans. He helped me find amazing collaborators who serve like I do. Sandy Wiles, Rachel Albritton, Madelyn Copperwaite, Chris Drouin, Betsy Wallace and Chanel Wells-Henderson are full of such talent and are willing to share it with me and the authors we get to serve. And Jennifer Crosswhite's editing skills helped bring this book to the masses.

I am grateful to each and every author I have had the honor of supporting. Every one of your stories has become a part of me. What I didn't know years ago, but I know now, is that no story can live in a silo. Every story is integrated with another. They overlap. They interweave. And in the process, they leave a piece of the author to become a piece of the reader.

I'll never measure emPact by the number of books I sell, the number of attendees at a speaking event or the number of engagements on social media posts. All I could ever hope is that my emPact can be measured by the small pieces of me I leave with those I meet.

EmPact may be finicky, but it's emPowering.

ABOUT THE AUTHOR

Stephanie Feger is "one of those" people who breathe, eat, sleep and dream book marketing. (Pathetic, right?!) She didn't realize how odd that was until an author once told her, "Stephanie, I'd rather scrub toilets than market my book." If she would have lived closer, Stephanie would have offered a trade because cleaning toilets is one thing she works hard to avoid.

Stephanie loves marketing, but not the icky marketing most people think about. Instead, she loves authentic marketing—the kind that helps connect people with something they didn't know they needed until they realize they can't live without it. She is passionate about helping people with an amazing message spread it. The world needs more of that, and she loves being a small part of that process.

She is also a lover of ongoing learning, and books give her the opportunity to deepen her knowledge base in the process. She believes every book she reads makes her a better person, and she embraces the honor she gets to read nearly every book the emPower PR Group supports. Speaking of which, she is the author of several books herself and is the founder, owner and chief strategist of the emPower PR Group, a boutique marketing solution for nonfiction authors.

She loves everything about what she does, but hearing her children tell others that she gets to work with the coolest people on the planet reminds her that letting go of her own plans and letting Life (or God, from her perspective) take over is totally worth it. Her favorite part of her work is meeting people vulnerable enough to share their stories in the hopes of inspiring others along the way. That takes great courage, and she cherishes that. She's met and helped people all over the world—with way cooler accents than her Kentucky one—and she is constantly excited to help them be successful.

One author told her, "Stephanie, I've figured out your MO. When I win, you win." That author was so right!

Stephanie, her husband Cory, and their three children—Eli, Lyndi and Luke—live on a twenty-five-acre farm in Kentucky where they have a zoo of cats—Baby, Timmy, Oreo, Snickers, Tom and Luna—and the sweetest dog on the planet, Zoey. When she isn't helping her clients, enjoying the cathartic release of writing herself or cutting grass at turbo speeds on the riding lawn mower, Stephanie enjoys hiking in the mountains of the Red River Gorge, going to the movies with her family and eating a whole bag of popcorn herself, and spending time reflecting on God's beauty in her every day.

Learn more about Stephanie Feger, the author, at StephanieFeger.com.

Learn more about how Stephanie and her team are a solution for authors by visiting emPowerPRGroup.com.

ABOUT THE EMPOWER PR GROUP

Originally the emPower PR Group was designed to emPower authors with the book marketing guidance they needed to be successful. Stephanie Feger knows most authors have limited budgets, and she wanted to make the biggest emPact for them.

She'll never forget, however, one of her first authors telling her, "Thank you, Stephanie, for emPowering me. I don't want to be emPowered anymore. Can I pay you to do the work?"

She laughed and realized there are three subsets of authors who could benefit from her knowledge, skillset and expertise:

- Those who want to learn and do it themselves. (They are the do-it-yourself authors.)
- Those who want to be emPowered and are seeking coaching and execution support in a way that they will learn the tricks of the trade at the same time. (Those are the do-it-with-me authors.)
- Those who have no desire to learn and just want it done. (Those are the do-it-for-me authors.)

The emPower PR Group continues to listen to the needs of nonfiction authors and offer solutions, no matter where they are in their book marketing journey:

- If you are an author looking for resources to help you roll up your sleeves and get it done, the emPower PR Group offers

free resources, a robust YouTube channel and weekly podcast episodes where authors can learn and run with their learning.
- If you are an author looking for immersive support, the emPower PR Group also offers programs and services for those who want one-on-one coaching and marketing execution.

In the evolution of the business, Stephanie has done a lot of listening, and she's identified three ways she and her team of marketing experts can best help authors (and it just so happens that this book is designed to support those three ways!):

- Many authors come to the emPower PR Group after their manuscript is written and handed off to publishers, but there is nothing worse than getting a book ready to market that isn't marketable. We offer solutions to fill in that gap.
- Launching a book is daunting, and many authors seek support in doing so. We offer solutions to help authors launch or relaunch their book to success.
- Most authors don't realize the moment they publish a book, they are launching a business, but we do! We offer solutions for authors who embrace their authorpreneurship but need some marketing guidance along the way.

The emPower PR Group helps authors write marketable books that will sell; promote their books to those who need them, want them, and will buy them; and build meaningful businesses around their emPowering messages. Together with her team, Stephanie develops customized marketing strategies and associated tactics to ensure those who need to hear of a message, a product, a book or a brand, do.

When is the best time to pull in marketing? Today. No joke. It's never too early or too late!

Learn more about the emPower PR Group at emPowerPRGroup.com.

ALSO BY STEPHANIE FEGER

Stephanie's first book, *Color Today Pretty: An Inspirational Guide to Living a Life in Perspective*, was the beginning of a new calling for her. It charged her to merge her love with her passion, and it continues to inspire her to always let perspective guide her way. Her second book, *Color Today Pretty Guided Journal*, is a complement to her first, inviting readers to invite her insights into their lives. Learn more by visiting StephanieFeger.com.

Color Today Pretty: An Inspirational Guide to Living a Life in Perspective

Through relatable and powerful true stories, Stephanie inspires you to live your own life more richly. Learn how to rise above disappointment or hardship, to prevent monotony from clouding your ability to savor profound moments, and to hold onto happiness and faith no matter what comes your way.

Color Today Pretty: An Inspirational Guide to Living a Life in Perspective, which debuted as an Amazon #1 best seller in its category, is more than a book—it's a way of living that underscores the need for compassion, curiosity and unwavering love. Come with Stephanie on an intimate walk of reflection and an exploration of how true perspective changes everything—including how we love, forgive, appreciate and awaken to new possibilities.

Color Today Pretty Guided Journal: A Personal Reflection Companion

Whether you have read or are currently reading *Color Today Pretty: An Inspirational Guide to Living a Life in Perspective* and are seeking to bring the words off the page and into your life, or you are looking for a tool to help you, your team, your group or your organization utilize for deeper reflection, this guided journal provides you structure for personal and group reflection, creative elements for unique learning and guidance to help you unpack the weight that you may currently be carrying.

The *Color Today Pretty Guided Journal* parallels the stories found within Stephanie's first book, but gives you the opportunity and the space to reflect on each. Your journey toward perspective awaits! Are you ready to take the leap to *color today pretty*?

Emergence: Living Lessons from the Soil

Life offers endless teachers. Some plant seeds of opportunities while others till the soil in preparation for sowing. Many create conditions for growth, and a select few become trusted advisors to prune our paths. There are people who nourish our growth and others who support in the reaping the harvest.

Everything in life is for a season and with a reason. For Stephanie, one of life's greatest teachers is the soil. She learned the value of sweat equity on her grandparents' farm as her family lived off and learned from the land. Her other grandma, who had more plants than apartment space, taught her the importance of patience, resilience and the interconnectedness of all living things.

At a young age, she unearthed the living lessons of the land, and with dirt under her nails, Stephanie continues to learn from her vegetable garden, house plants and farm what it takes to cultivate a fulfilling life.

Emergence: Living Lessons from the Soil provides a treasure trove of inspiration and guidance for those seeking to find beauty in the mess, power in the mundane and meaning in the drought. Like we would a garden, we must nurture ourselves too.

www.ingramcontent.com/pod-product-compliance
Lightning Source LLC
Chambersburg PA
CBHW072048110526
44590CB00018B/3089